Thaddeus Allen

Facts Illustrative of the Practical Tendencies of the Distinctive Views, Principles, Agencies, and Influences

of the leading men in the origination of the American Union, and in the

formation and successive administrations of the Government

Thaddeus Allen

Facts Illustrative of the Practical Tendencies of the Distinctive Views, Principles, Agencies, and Influences
of the leading men in the origination of the American Union, and in the formation and successive administrations of the Government

ISBN/EAN: 9783337311704

Printed in Europe, USA, Canada, Australia, Japan

Cover: Foto ©Suzi / pixelio.de

More available books at **www.hansebooks.com**

FACTS

ILLUSTRATIVE OF THE

PRACTICAL T NDENCIES

OF THE

DISTINCTIVE VIEWS, PRINCIPLES, AGENCIES, AND INFLUENCES

OF THE

LEADING MEN

IN THE ORIGINATION OF THE

AMERICAN UNION,

AND IN THE

FORMATION AND SUCCESSIVE ADMINISTRATIONS

OF

THE GOVERNMENT.

BY THADDEUS ALLEN, A.M.

TRUTH OUR AIM : FACTS OUR GUIDE.

BOSTON:
PRATT BROTHERS, PRINTERS, 37½ CORNHILL.
1868.

[NOTE. — *These first eight pages were prepared, and intended to be published by themselves, in* 1866.]

IN this year of our Lord, 1866, the alarmingly complicated derangements in the vital affairs of the Nation, and the conflicting views and opinions of its Rulers respecting their cause and their remedy, so much resemble those recorded in the latest and most disheartening years of the Confederation, that the question naturally arises — a question now of special public interest — whether these existing derangements, and those so recorded, really had, as they appear to have had, one and the same paternity; and, if so, when and in what manner were first manifested the agencies and influences which caused them?

Considering the late urgent and frequent appeals to the people of the United States to maintain and preserve the Constitution as it is, thus assuming it to be perfect in all its parts; and considering, also, that those appeals are made while the Government — administered professedly according to its sanctioned provisions — is in so unsettled and precarious a condition as to produce deep anxiety and agitation throughout the country, it seems to be quite time to inquire with more care and discrimination into the origin and nature of the two sections in that incomparable Charter of the Fathers, which relate to the election of Representatives to Congress.

The expediency of this can hardly fail to be perceived by every one who realizes the fact, that the characteristic tendency and legitimate results of the transfer of national power from Congress to the several States, by those two Sections, are now being clearly, and, to many at least, most calamitously illustrated by "*my policy*" in the administration of the Government.

In aid of the inquiry alluded to, it may be stated that, on the 24th of July, the memorable Convention of 1787 appointed five of their members a committee, called by them the Committee of Detail, to more suitably arrange their "proceedings for the establishment of a National Government."

At the opening of their business, May 29th, Mr. Charles Pinckney, of South Carolina, offered a series of propositions in a form similar to that of the Constitution; and, on the 26th of July, the Convention referred those propositions of MR. PINCKNEY, together with their previously adopted Resolutions, to that Committee of Detail appointed "to prepare and report a Constitution conformable thereto." In the twenty-three Resolutions so referred, the following is all that related to the manner of electing those Representatives: —

"*Resolved*, That the first branch of the [National] Legislature ought to be elected by the people of the several States, for the term of two years."

Below are the propositions of MR. PINCKNEY on the subject.

ARTICLE III. — " The members of the House of Delegates [Representatives] shall be chosen every —— year by the people of the several States, and the qualifications of electors shall be the same as those of the electors in the several States for their Legislatures."

ARTICLE V. — " Each State shall prescribe the time and manner of holding eléctions by the people for the House of Delegates [Representatives]."

Next are those two Sections in the Constitution.

ARTICLE I., *Section 2d.* — " The House of Representatives shall be composed of members chosen every second year, by the people of the several States; and the electors in each State shall have the qualifications requisite for electors of the most numerous branch of the State Legislature."

Section 4th, of the same Article. — " The times, places, and manner of holding elections for Senators and Representatives, shall be prescribed in each State by the Legislature thereof; but the Congress may at any time, by law, make or alter such regulations, except as to the place of choosing Senators."

If these two sections are accurately compared with the above Resolution, and with MR. PINCKNEY'S Articles (3d and 5th), there could seemingly be little doubt in what quarter their objectionable features originated. MR. RUTLEDGE, likewise of South Carolina, was a member of that Committee of Detail. They delivered in their Report, August 6th.

When the last clause of Section 4th was taken up in the Convention (the clause appended by the Committee to MR. PINCKNEY'S Article 5th), " MR. PINCKNEY and MR. RUTLEDGE moved to strike it out. The States, they contended, could and must be relied on in such cases."

If these immediately preceding facts are considered jointly with the result of such comparison, there could seem to remain no doubt that those objectionable features originated in the deep-seated and too lasting jealousies and prejudices of the notoriously erratic State of South Carolina. Had their consequences been limited to that period of time, and to the comparatively unimportant territory of that single State, it would have been a matter of little interest to the great American Republic, to trace those consequences; but since they have not only continued, but so increased and prevailed through the whole Southern portion of the Union, and still exist by far too extensively in the Northern, it seems a matter of *general interest*, to direct attention to the manner in which some of the other members of that Convention, then representing a majority of the people, regarded the tendency of those two Sections, even as they were suffered to stand in the Constitution

As already mentioned, the Committee of Detail reported to the Convention, August 6th.

August 7th. — Section 2d, requiring that "the electors in each State shall have the qualifications requisite for electors of the most numerous branch of the State Legislature," being taken up, the member who reported it argued, that "it was difficult to form any uniform rule of qualifications for the States. Unnecessary innovations, he thought, too, should be avoided."

MR. GOUVERNEUR MORRIS [of Pennsylvania], after answering the arguments used in support of it, added, "Another objection against the clause, as it stands, is, that it makes the qualifications for the National Legislature depend on the will of the States, which he thought not proper."

August 8th. — The Convention taking up the part of Section 2d concerning the prerequisite residence for a member of the House of Representatives, "MR. RUTLEDGE urged and moved that a residence of seven years should be required *in the State* wherein the member should be elected. An emigrant from New England to South Carolina or Georgia could know little of its affairs, and could not be supposed to acquire a thorough knowledge, in less time."

"MR. GEORGE READ [of Delaware] reminded him that we were now forming a *National* Government, and that such a regulation would correspond little with the idea that we were one people."

"MR. JAMES WILSON [of Pennsylvania] enforced the same consideration."

MR. JOHN FRANCIS MERCER * [of Maryland]. — "Such a regulation would present a greater alienship than existed under the old Federal system. It would interweave local jealousies and State distinctions in the very Constitution which is meant to cure them."

August 9th. — It was on that day that Section 4th, respecting "The times, places, etc., came under consideration, as mentioned before, when MR. PINCKNEY and MR. RUTLEDGE moved to strike out the last clause, contending that the States "could and must be relied on in such cases."

MR. NATHANIEL GORHAM [of Massachusetts]. — "It would be as improper to take this power from the National Legislature as to restrain the British Parliament from regulating

* Mr. Mercer took his seat in the Convention, *Aug. 6th.*

the circumstances of elections, leaving this business to the counties themselves."

MR. JAMES MADISON [of Virginia]. — "The necessity of a General Government . . . . . seems to decide that the Legislatures of the States ought not to have the uncontrolled right of regulating the times, places, and manner, of holding elections. These were words of great latitude. It was impossible to foresee all the abuses that might be made of such discretionary power [in the States]. . . . . It seemed as improper in principle, though it might be less inconvenient in practice, to give to the State Legislatures this great authority over the election of the Representatives of the people in the General Legislature, as it would be to give to the latter a like power over the election of their Representatives in the State Legislature."

MR. RUFUS KING [of Massachusetts]. — "If this power be not given to the National Legislature, their right of judging of the returns of their members may be frustrated. . . . Although the scheme of erecting the General Government on the authority of the State Legislatures has been fatal to the Federal establishment, it would seem as if many gentlemen still fostered the dangerous idea."

The above extracts from MR. MADISON's "Journal of Debates in the Convention" indicate clearly that both classes of the members equally considered the *Legislative*, as the department of Government to be possessed of the entire and exclusive authority over those elections. On that subject, therefore, the only question between them was, whether that authority should be vested in the National Legislature, to secure the requisite uniformity through all parts of the Union; or whether the conditions of those elections should be subjected to the control of the discordant jealousies and prejudices of the several State Legislatures.

Thus, the issue between them appears to have been of the same nature as that now pending between Congress and the President, — the same as was manifested through the whole course of the debates in the Convention, — and, indeed, of the same nature as that which has in varied degrees disturbed and agitated the Republic, from the autumn of 1775, to the present time.

Who can tell the number or amount of the wide-spreading evils which have been experienced in that period, from the excess of power in the States, acquired principally by their own assumptions, but in no small measure by the too great concessions to them in parts of the Constitution?

Fortunately, Congress have so perceived some of those evils, now most imminent, that they have attempted the only effectual remedy, by proposing a necessary amendment to the time-honored Charter of National Freedom.

That such a measure has become necessary, can admit of no fair question or doubt, when we consider the above two sections in the Constitution with reference to a peculiar policy recently adopted to restore to their former relations in the Union the people of the territory lately in rebellion — against the nation.

Without some preliminary measure to effectually prevent further mischiefs from those two sections, an attempt to bring them into the Union by the action of those artificial beings called States, — as they went out, — rather than by the action of the loyal portion of the inhabitants of that territory, would be virtually an attempt to surrender to the States the power and duty of the National Government to defend and protect those inhabitants, and thereby to expose them to whatever persecutions and cruelties their treasonable neighbors and State Legislatures might be prompted to inflict upon them. It would be, moreover, at once to relinquish all the security that has been gained by the immense sacrifices of blood and treasure in the war, and to renew the liability to a repetition of like calamities in future.

Few as are the preceding extracts from the debates, they indicate the too generally unregarded fact, that in 1787, as well as before and since, there were in the United States two distinct classes of patriotic statesmen, — early divided from each other by their different conceptions as to the kind of principle whereon to form a plan or system of government, and of all general operations, either civil or military, best calculated to meet the various accumulating new and untried exigencies, all of which they had been selected to provide for.

They indicate no less intelligibly, also, that the members of one of those classes directed their attention and care chiefly to local or State concerns, and earnestly and too successfully labored to transfer to the States essential powers which the general welfare required to be possessed and exercised by the National Government; and that the other class, — whether in or out of the convention, — while recognizing the importance of State authorities, regarded them as subordinate and auxiliary to the infinitely more important whole; and, accordingly, believing the substantial interests of the States to be best provided for by securing the interests of the people composing them, they exerted strenuously and perseveringly their utmost energies for the establishment of a National Government, of adequate efficacy, stability, and permanency, to secure the peace and freedom of all the people in all the States.

The records show, that the principle of this latter class was adopted as fundamental in the formation of the Union, in 1774; that it was observed as the basis of all plans of operation in the military department during the war for Independence; and that the wisest, ablest, and most experienced statesmen of that period, regarded it as the true principle of the Union and Government, till the close of their lives   It is likewise shown by the records, that the principle of the former class, the class above represented by Mr. Pinckney and Mr. Rutledge, was first publicly manifested in the autumn of 1775; that it originated in the peculiar conceptions of a few then leading members of Congress, whose mental bias and prejudice prompted them to renounce the principle of Union on which they had unitedly begun, and, thus seceding from their colleagues, to adopt as the basis of their system, a principle far different in its stead.   That was the first actual secession in the United States, and the first practical application of the principle on which has since been claimed a *right* of nullification and secession.

That justly celebrated band of Patriots was in that manner sundered into two political classes or parties.

Thenceforward, for years, there were practically employed in conducting public operations two distinct systems, which were soon found to be — and they continued so to be through the stupendous war of Revolution — as widely divergent in tendency as they were palpably different in principle.

It should be observed that each of those principles was applied in directing public affairs — one in the military, the other in the civil department— long before the theory founded on either of them was formed into a system of government.

The one thus and then adopted prevailed in the administration of those affairs in the civil department, from that time till the organization of the government under the Constitution, in 1789.

The speedily resulting derangements, extending to every public department, and almost continually increasing to their consummation in the awfully anarchical condition of the country in 1787, so thoroughly convinced the people of the radical defect and perilous tendency of the system, that a majority of them firmly resolved to abandon altogether the principle on which it had been founded, and to substitute the principle of the other system.   For that purpose they called forth those ever memorable benefactors, who had been first and foremost in achieving Independence, as the class most reliable for counsel and guidance, and most competent to regulate and secure the freedom which they had so nobly won; and the event proved the wisdom of their course.

Opposed in the Convention as in the war of Revolution, by a class numerically scarcely less than their own, that now imperfectly appreciated class whose chief was Washington, by oft-repeated and persistent efforts during more than three months, so far succeeded, in spite of such opposition, as to restore to the Union the amount of self-sustaining and conservative power there is in the Constitution.

Called afterward to administer the government which they had so largely contributed to form and establish, they "as by magic" raised the then existing generation from the very verge of bewildering anarchy to a condition of peace, order, and prosperity.

So then, as always, the direct tendency of the former system was, to disarrange and subvert; that of the latter, to regulate and establish. These truths the people of that period thoroughly and practically learned, by their impressive experiences of the opposite results from the two systems; and, in so learning them, they learned what counsels and examples to confide in and follow, and what to distrust and avoid. Unutterably fortunate it was for themselves, and for the successive generations after them, that they at the same time learned how to relieve and save their then greatly depressed and imperiled country.

Much as it should be regretted, the main facts, especially those relating to that period, have been so perverted or obscured by many writers and speakers respecting the nature and formation of the American Union and Government, that only through the original records can be obtained the practical knowledge of those experiences, which guided the people so well *then*, and which is exceedingly needful, if not indispensable, to guide the people as well *now*, in 1866.

Viewing the foregoing facts in connection with the remarkable political experiences of this year, and of several preceding years, it would seem that intelligent patriotism might be prompted to more efficient and persevering endeavors to distinguish the respective agencies and influences of the two classes, and their respective bearings upon the great interests of the country.

But few seem to know, or care to inquire, whether the Government of the United States has been administered by FRANKLIN PIERCE, JAMES BUCHANAN, and ANDREW JOHNSON, more in accordance with the true, original principle of the Union and the Constitution, than with that of the previous system, called the Confederation ; or, in other words, whether it has been administered by them more in accordance with the political theory of GEORGE WASHINGTON than with that of THOMAS JEFFERSON.

However regarded, here is suggested a distinction, on the observance of which depend, as hitherto and ever, the vital interests, the peace, the security and prosperity of the American nation. It is a distinction which every one in a position of influence in the Government ought to be able to promptly and truly define. No American statesman or citizen should pretend to possess a practical knowledge of the political history of his country, unless he has accurately learned the distinctive tendency of each of those theories, as that tendency has been developed by its results in the

successive generations since the commencement of the
Union. As long as he is unable to so mark those tendencies respectively, as to clearly distinguish each from the
other, so long the plain teachings of his nation's varied experiences will appear to him confused and unintelligible, and,
therefore, afford no practical guidance.

Pending the preposterous war of rebellion, its horrors
were greatly alleviated in the minds of the very many, who
confidently anticipated as a consequence the long-needed
correction of that radical error in the public sentiment of
the people, and in the public measures of their rulers, which,
stealthily increasing and advancing, had given birth to the
attempt of a State to nullify laws of the United States, and,
remaining still uncorrected, had at length misled a confiding
nation even to a condition so terrific and calamitous.

But the multiplied complications in the vastly momentous
concerns of the country since the close of actual war, and
some of the schemes proposed for regulating and adjusting
them, indicate too plainly that such anticipations are yet far
from being realized, and that there is now no little occasion
for a renewal of the knowledge and application of those lessons of warning as well as of encouragement, which were so
thoroughly and practically learned from the widely-different
experiences in the first quarter of a century from the nation's
beginning,—that fundamental period of American institutions.

Those different or rather opposite experiences, considered
then as the unmistakable evidences of the specific tendency
of the theory or principle from which they respectively resulted, were regarded by that generation as the true and infalli-
ble lessons for political guidance, not only in that period but
in all the subsequent periods of independent America.

Those lessons, however, are not imparted or acquired by
now and then quoting indiscriminately some of those memorable men, who collectively are justly regarded as Fathers
of the Revolution. Indiscriminate references to those fathers must appear of little significance to every one who
knows the fact, that, on a near view of an absolute and final
separation from Great Britain, no inconsiderable number of
them, from their peculiar mental bias and temperament, as
already shown, renounced the national principle on which
they had all begun, and adopted another. *Adequate knowledge of those lessons is possessed by only those who have
correctly learned the distinctive tendency of each of those
principles, which those two classes of patriots, whether in the
cabinet or field, respectively adopted as its peculiar basis of
every public arrangement.

May the people gain such knowledge from the original
records to be found in subsequent pages, and then practically
apply it as wisely for present and future exigencies as did
the generation of that period.†

But the increased and still increasing complications in national affairs, in 1867, '68, and the no less conflicting opinions and plans for regulating and adjusting them, when viewed with reference to the seemingly unnoticed cause from which they mainly proceeded, appear to afford little prospect of enduring advance in that direction, till the people and their rulers so learn the distinctive character of the agencies and influences of the several leading men in the birth-period of the Nation, that they may be enabled to fully and practically understand how those renowned patriots respectively affected the nature of the Union, — whether for good, or whether for evil, — first, in the various stages of the Revolution, then in the formation of the Constitution, and again in the administration of the Government.

To be satisfied of the infinite importance of possessing and disseminating such knowledge throughout every section of the country, requires only to adequately conceive how clearly the widely different political views and influences, which agitate the nation so deeply now, are traceable to their origin and their respective authors in that period wherein so vastly diverse plans of general operations were formed.

That the same influences, unchanged in character, though successively varied in relative degrees, have descended through the generations, to the present time, cannot be truthfully denied or reasonably doubted.

The great misfortune has been, that those tending to disturb, disorganize, and unsettle, have too often and too much prevailed over those which invariably tend to tranquillize, regulate, and establish.

In this connection, some may recollect the significant fact, that, both during the still-continued precarious condition of the nation, and through the long course of influences and events which led to it, not only reputed politicians, but respected orators, editors, and even honored historians and biographers, have repeatedly and most emphatically cited, *as model Statesmen,* some of the most prominent members of that class of the fathers, who have been twice referred to as the authors of that system,* which twelve years' experience of its legitimate results taught the people of 1787 to entirely abandon and repudiate, as constantly tending to political confusion and disaster.

Though so much to be lamented, such radically misguiding exhibitions will excite little wonder, so far as the fact is known and considered, that, mainly for prudential reasons, which will appear in these pages, the most essential truths relating to that period were never so clearly and fully explained, as to be practically understood by even the generation which next succeeded it.

Hence, in very many of the writings and speeches on the

* See pages 6 and 7.

subject, — especially in the latter portion of them, — error
is so extensively blended with the most important truths, or
those truths are so partially presented — often quite perverted — that, practically, as regards the distinctive counsels
and examples of those two classes of Statesmen, the last has
too nearly become the first; and the first, last.

In view of these truths, it would seem, that both justice to
them, and a due regard for the present and future interests
of the nation, demand a more discriminate and thorough
knowledge of their respective agencies and influences as the
records show them. Toward this necessary attainment, the
first lesson to be learned, is, that those two classes were sev-
erally characterized by the particular principle of the system
of operations which they respectively originated or persist-
ently advocated; for it is only by previously learning their
characteristics, as thus distinguished from each other, that
those of their respective followers, in this or in any other period
subsequent to that first, can be so clearly distinguished as to
afford the practical guidance which has long been needed
— and which is now especially needed — for extricating the
great affairs of the nation from their present alarmingly multiplied derangements and difficulties.

Yet, pressing as are the various exigencies of those affairs,
few if any seem to know there was ever such an event as
that division among the country's chosen Guardians, mentioned in the preceding pages (6th and 7th). That event,
however, occurring at so early and critical a stage of the
Revolution, — and involving, at the same time, an entire departure from the principle on which the public operations had
been from the beginning to that time directed, — was productive of consequences, which, in magnitude and extent, have
greatly exceeded those of any other political event in the
whole history of the Union.

By it, as has been shown, that august Assembly was sundered into two political classes or parties. Although appar-
ently unknown, or unthought of, for many years past, the
political distinction thus and then originated was thenceforward carefully observed by each party, as of such vital importance for the salvation of the country, that it was the very
pivot on which were suspended all the political vibrations
during a half century, from the first public manifestation of
it in the autumn of 1775.

As that division among them arose entirely from their different views and plans for meeting occasions which were
then all new to them, it would seem reasonable to suppose
them to have been at that time equally honest and patriotic;
but the widely variant practical tendencies and results of
their different plans soon indicated, and prolonged experience
has fully proved, that those two classes were far from being
equally sagacious and wise in directing their endeavors to

provide for the permanent freedom and welfare of their country.

The following extracts are referred to, as affording some just idea of the circumstances, nature, and extent of the earliest portion of the consequences experienced from that division : —

GENERAL GREENE wrote to Gov. WARD, in Congress, *Oct.* 16, 1775, — " With regard to paying the troops part of their wages, and the Committee part, it will be productive of a multitude of inconveniences. . . . . As the troops are considered Continental, and not Colonial, there must be some systematical plan for the payment, without reference to any particular Colonies.

. " His Excellency has a great desire to banish every idea of local attachments. . . . For my part, I feel the cause, and not the place."

HON. THOMAS LYNCH, in Congress, to GENERAL WASHINGTON, *Nov.*, 1775. —" With grief and shame, it must be confessed, that the whole blame lies not with the army. You will find your hands straitened instead of strengthened. What the event will be, it is impossible to foresee ; perhaps it is only intended to force the Continent into their own terms, and to show that neither General nor Congress [but the Colonies] shall be permitted to control the army."

GENERAL WASHINGTON, to COLONEL READ, *Nov.* 28, 1775. — " Could I have foreseen what I have experienced, and am likely to experience, no consideration upon earth should have induced me to accept this command."

GENERAL WASHINGTON, to the PRESIDENT OF CONGRESS, *Dec.* 14, 1775. — " The resolves relative to captures made by Continental armed vessels, only want a court established for trial to make them complete. This I hope will soon be done, as I have taken the liberty to urge it often to the Congress."

Yet, on the 20th, Congress passed the resolve, that such cases should be libelled in the Courts of Admiralty erected in the Colonies.

GENERAL GREENE, to GOVERNOR WARD, in Congress, *Dec.* 31, 1775. — " How unhappy for the interests of America, that such colonial prejudices should prevail, and partial motives influence her councils ! If they are nourished, they will sooner or later sap the foundation of the Union. . . God in mercy avert so dreadful an evil."

GENERAL WASHINGTON, to the PRESIDENT OF CONGRESS, *Sept.* 24, 1776. — " The wounds which my feelings, as an officer, have received by a thousand things that have happened, contrary to my expectations and wishes, . . . added to a consciousness of my inability to govern an army composed of such discordant parts, — induce not only the belief, but a thorough conviction in my mind, that it will be impossible, unless there is a thorough change in our military system, for me to conduct matters in such a manner as to give satisfaction to the public."

GENERAL GREENE, to ———, *Sept.* 28, 1776. — " The policy of Congress has been the most absurd and ridiculous imaginable. . . . A military force established upon such principles defeats itself. . . . The Congress goes upon a penurious plan."

GENERAL WASHINGTON, to the PRESIDENT OF CONGRESS, *Oct.* 4, 1776. — "And I see such a distrust and jealousy of military power, that the Commander-in-Chief has not an opportunity, even by recommendation, to give the least assurances of reward for the most essential services. In a word, such a cloud of perplexing circumstances appears before me, without one flattering hope, that I am thoroughly convinced that unless the most vigorous and decisive exertions are immediately adopted to remedy these evils, the certain and absolute loss of our liberties will be the inevitable consequence."

The eccentric GENERAL CHARLES LEE, to GENERAL GATES, *Oct.* 14, 1776. — "*Inter nos*, Congress seem to stumble at every step." . . . General Washington is much to blame in not menacing them with resignation, unless they refrain from unhinging the army by their absurd interference."

GENERAL WASHINGTON, to J. A. WASHINGTON, *Nov.* 19, 1776. — "I am wearied almost to death with the retrograde motion of things, and solemnly protest, that a pecuniary reward of twenty thousand pounds a year would not induce me to undergo what I do ; and, after all, perhaps to lose my character, as it is impossible, under such a variety of distressing circumstances, to conduct matters agreeably to public expectation, or even to the expectation of those [Congress] who employ me, as they will not make proper allowances for the *difficulties their own errors have occasioned.*"

SAME, to the PRESIDENT OF CONGRESS, *Dec.* 20, 1776. — "I can only add, that desperate diseases require desperate remedies. . . . My feelings, as an officer and a man, have been such as to force me to say, that no person ever had a greater choice of difficulties to contend with than I have.

.   .   .   .   .   .

"That I have labored, ever since I have been in the service, to discourage all kinds of local attachments and distinctions of country, denominating the whole by the greater name of AMERICAN. But I have found it impossible to overcome prejudices."

ROBERT MORRIS, in Congress, to GENERAL WASHINGTON, *Dec.* 23, 1776. — "It is useless, at this period, to examine into the causes of our present unhappy situation, unless that examination would be productive of a cure for the evils which surround us. In fact, those causes have long been known to such as would open their eyes. The very consequences of them were foretold, and the measures execrated, by some of the best friends of America ; but in vain, . . . and nothing is now left but to extricate ourselves as well as we can."

Thus are indicated, in the language of some of those who best knew and most deeply felt them, a portion of the early consequences of that substitution of a wholly different principle of plan for directing public affairs, at so critical and momentous a juncture.

It is proper to notice, that, to the extent indicated by the preceding extracts, those consequences became embarrassing. and imperiling throughout both the civil and military departments, in little more than one year after that most extraordinary change (or reverse) of public policy.

As may have been already inferred, that change was a natural result of the excessive State attachment, State jealousy and prejudice, of a few then leading members of Congress. By their influence, at the time, that venerated Council were induced to adopt the new principle as the rule of their proceedings, and, in 1776, to erect upon it that impracticable structure called the Confederation, — the system of government formed by Congress to achieve, and to render perpetually secure, the independence, freedom, harmony, and prosperity, of all the people comprehended in the American Union.

Accordingly, as that system and all the proceedings of Congress were based on the same State or Confederate principle, the direction of public affairs, in the civil department, was, from that juncture, little affected or varied, either

by the Declaration of Independence, by the completion of
the form of that system, in November, 1777, or by the final
acceptance and ratification of it, in March, 1781. Indeed,
the same general direction was continued by Congress till
the necessity for the Constitutional Convention of 1787 became manifest to all, and to none more so than to Congress
themselves.

The evidences of some of the later consequences of that
change are found in the following extracts : —

GENERAL GREENE, to ———, *June* 4, 1777. — "Wisdom and prudence
sometimes forsake the wisest bodies. I am exceedingly distressed at the
state of things in the great National Council."

GENERAL WASHINGTON, to R. H. LEE, in Congress, *Oct.* 17, 1777. — "To
sum up the whole, I have been a slave to the service. I have undergone
more than most men are aware of, to harmonize so many discordant parts."

GENERAL WASHINGTON, to BENJAMIN HARRISON, in the House of Delegates, Va., *Dec.* 18, 1778. — "My conception of the matter impresses it
too strongly upon me that the States, separately, are too much engaged
in their local concerns. . . . In a word, I think our political system
may be compared to the mechanism of a clock, and that we should derive
a lesson from it; for it answers no good purpose to keep the smaller wheels
in order, if the greater one, which is the support and prime mover of the
whole, is neglected."

SAME, to JOSEPH JONES, in Congress, *May* 31, 1780. — "We can no
longer drudge on in the old way. . . We are always working up-hill.
. . . I see one head gradually changing into thirteen. I see one army
branching into thirteen, . . and I am fearful of the consequences."

LAFAYETTE wrote, in his "Memoirs," — "The pecuniary succors [ob-
tained by him from France] were placed at the disposal of General Washington ; for it was upon that General that reposed the whole confidence of
the Government, and the hopes of the French nation."

GENERAL WASHINGTON, to JOHN MATTHEWS, in Congress, *Oct.* 4, 1780. —
"But, knowing the jealousies which have been entertained on this head
(Heaven knows how unjustly), and *that the political helm was in another
direction*, I forbore to express my sentiments for a time; but, at a moment
when we are tottering on the brink of a precipice, silence would have been
criminal." *

SAME, to JOHN PARK CUSTIS, in the House of Delegates, Va., *Feb.* 28,
1781. — "In a word, . . we have brought a cause, which might have
been happily terminated years ago by the adoption of proper measures,
to the very verge of ruin."

SAME, to COLONEL A. HAMILTON, in Congress, *March* 31, 1783. — "I
rejoice most exceedingly that there is an end of our warfare, and that such
a field is opening to our view as will — with wisdom to cultivate it —
make us a great, a respectable, and a happy people; but it must be
improved by other means than State politics and unreasonable jealousies
and prejudices. . . . My wish to see the union of these States established upon liberal and permanent principles, and inclination to contribute
my mite in pointing out the defects of the present Constitution [Confed-
eration], are equally great." † . . For, to the defects thereof, . . may
justly be ascribed the prolongation of the war, and consequently the
expenses occasioned by it. More than half the perplexities I have experienced in the course of my command, and almost the whole of the difficulties and distress of the army, have had their origin here."

* Alluding to a very plain and emphatic letter he had written to Congress, on
the 20th of the preceding August.

† *Equally great* as that expressed in a letter he had shortly before received
from Col. Hamilton, relating to the same subject.

SAME, to BENJAMIN HARRISON, Governor of Virginia. — "The disinclination of the individual States to yield competent powers to Congress, . . . their unreasonable jealousy of that body and of one another, and the disposition, which seems to pervade each, of being all-wise and all-powerful within itself, will, if there is not a change in the system, be our downfall as a nation. This is as clear to me as A, B, C; and I think we have opposed Great Britain, and have arrived at the present state of independency, to very little purpose, if we cannot conquer our own prejudices."

SAME, to HON. JOHN JAY, *May* 18, 1786. — "I coincide perfectly with you, my dear sir, that there are errors in our National Government which call for correction, loudly, I would add. : . . We are certainly in a delicate situation. . . . To be plainer, I think there is more wickedness than ignorance mixed in our councils. Under this impression, I scarcely know what opinion to entertain of a general Convention. . . . Yet, something must be done, or the fabric must fall, for it is certainly tottering.
"Ignorance and design are difficult to combat."

SAME, to WILLIAM GRAYSON, in Congress, *July* 26, 1786. — "In a word, . . . our character as a nation is dwindling; and what it must come to, if a change should not soon take place, our enemies have foretold; for, in truth, we seem either not capable, or not willing, to take care of ourselves."

SAME, to JOHN JAY, *Aug.* 1, 1786. — "Your sentiments — that our affairs are drawing rapidly to a crisis — accord with my own. What the event will be, is also beyond my foresight. We have errors to correct. . . . I do not conceive we can exist long as a nation, without having lodged somewhere a power, which will pervade the whole Union in as energetic a manner as the authority of the State Governments extends over the several States.
"To be fearful of investing Congress with ample powers for national purposes, appears to me the very climax of popular absurdity and madness. . . . . Requisitions are actually little better than a jest and a by-word throughout the land. If you tell the Legislatures [of the States] they have violated the treaty of peace, and invaded the prerogatives of the Confederacy, they will laugh in your face. What, then, is to be done?"

SAME, to BUSHROD WASHINGTON, *Nov.* 15, 1786 — "Among the great objects which you took into consideration, at Richmond, how comes it to pass, that you never turned your eyes to the inefficacy of the Federal Government?* . . . Every man, who considers the present constitution of it, and sees to what it is verging, trembles. The fabric, which took nine years, at the expense of much blood and treasure, to rear, now totters to the foundation, and without support, must soon fall."

In Mr. Madison's introduction to his report of the debates in the Convention of 1787, he says, respecting the condition of the country : —

"Among the defects which had been severely felt, was want of an uniformity in cases requiring it, — as laws of naturalization and bankruptcy, a coercive authority operating on individuals, a guaranty of the internal tranquillity of the States."
"As a natural consequence of this distracted condition of the Union, the Federal authority had ceased to be respected abroad; and . . . at home, it had lost all confidence and credit, . . . involving a general decay of confidence and credit between man and man. . . . .
Such were the defects, the deformities, the diseases, and the ominous prospects, for which the Convention were to provide a remedy, and which

* A reference to the objects of that meeting at Richmond, as described by B. Washington, in a letter to the General.

ought never to be overlooked in expounding and appreciating the Constitutional Charter, the remedy that was provided."

OPENING OF THE CONVENTION.

Again, in the language of MR. MADISON, —

" GOVERNOR RANDOLPH [of Virginia], in an address, May 29th, at the opening of the main business of the Convention [of which he was a member], reviewed the danger of our situation, and appealed to the sense of the best friends of the United States — to the prospect of anarchy, from the laxity of government everywhere."

Relative to the above-mentioned address, the late CHIEF JUSTICE YATES, of New York, — who was also a member, and kept a journal, — says, under the same date, May 29th : —

" He [Gov. RANDOLPH] closed these remarks with a set of Resolutions, — fifteen in number, — which he proposed to the Convention for their adoption, and as leading principles whereon to form a new Government. He candidly confessed, that they were not intended for a Federal Government. He meant a strong, consolidated Union, in which the idea of States should be nearly annihilated. He then moved, that they should be taken up in Committee of the whole House."

JUDGE YATES says, further, that —

" MR. CHARLES PINCKNEY [a member from South Carolina] then added, that he had reduced his ideas of a new Government to a system, which he read ; and confessed that it was grounded on the same principle as that of the above Resolutions." *

IN CONVENTION, *May* 30th. — The following Resolutions were taken under consideration : —

" That a union of the States merely *federal* will not accomplish the objects proposed by the Articles of Confederation, namely, common defence, security of liberty, and general welfare.

" That a National Government ought to be established, consisting of a supreme Legislative, Executive, and Judiciary."

It seems proper to pause here, and to inquire whether there is found in the preceding pages enough to convey some just idea of the apparent want of aptitude and consistency in the administration of civil affairs, and of the consequent declension of those affairs till they were reduced to the very verge of hopeless degradation and anarchy.

An attempt will now be made, through an abridgment of MR. MADISON'S Report of the Debates, to show by what agencies and influences those affairs were quickly extricated from their extreme complications, and raised to an unprecedented condition of order, harmony, and prosperity throughout the land.

BEGINNING OF THE DEBATES.

The Resolution concerning the rights of suffrage in the National Legislature, being taken up, —

" MR. MADISON [from Virginia] observed that, . . . as the acts of the General Government would take effect without an intervention of the State

* See expressions of General Washington, in his letter to Mr. Jay, *Aug.* 1, 1783, p. 14.

Legislatures, . . . there was the same reason for different numbers of Representatives from different States, as from counties of different extents within particular States."

May 31st. — The Resolution, — "That the members of the first branch of the National Legislature ought to be elected by the people of the several States," — being taken up, —

"Mr. SHERMAN [from Connecticut] opposed the election by the people. . . . The people, he said, immediately, should have as little to do as may be about the Government. They want information, and are constantly liable to be misled."

"Mr. GERRY [from Massachusetts]. — The evils we experience flow from the excess of democracy. The people do not want virtue, but are the dupes of pretended patriots. . . . He said he was still republican; but had been taught by experience the danger of the levelling spirit."

"Mr. JAMES WILSON [from Pennsylvania] contended strenuously for drawing the most numerous branch immediately from the people. . . On examination, it would be found that the opposition of States to Federal measures had proceeded much more from the officers of the States than from the people at large."

"Mr. MADISON considered the popular election of one branch of the National Legislature as essential to every plan of free government."

The clause of the Resolution, "authorizing an exertion of the force of the whole against a delinquent State," coming under consideration, —

"Mr. MADISON. — The use of force against a State would look more like a declaration of war, than an infliction of punishment, and would probably be considered by the party attacked as a dissolution of all previous compacts by which it might be bound. *He hoped that such a system would be framed as might render this resource unnecessary.*"

June 6th. — "Mr. GEORGE REED [from Delaware]. — Too much attachment is betrayed to the State Governments. . . If we do not establish a good Government, on new principles, we must either go to ruin, or have the work to do over again. The people at large are wrongly suspected of being averse to a General Government. The aversion lies among interested men who possess their confidence."

June 8th. — "Mr. CHARLES PINCKNEY moved, that the National Legislature should have authority to negative all laws which they should judge to be improper. He urged that such a universality of the power was indispensably necessary to render it effectual; . . . that, if the States were left to act of themselves in any case, it would be impossible to defend the National prerogatives, however extensive they might be, on paper."

"Mr. MADISON seconded the motion. Experience had evinced a constant tendency in the States to encroach on the Federal authority; to violate national treaties; to infringe the rights and interests of each other. . . . A negative was the mildest expedient that could be devised for preventing these mischiefs. The existence of such a check would prevent attempts to commit them. Should no such precaution be engrafted, the only remedy would be an appeal to coercion. Was such a remedy eligible? . . . . *Any government for the United States, formed on the supposed practicability of using force against the unconstitutional proceedings of the States, would prove as visionary and fallacious as the government of Congress.* The negative would render the use of force unnecessary. . . . . In a word, . . this prerogative of the General Government is the great pervading principle that must control the centrifugal tendency of the States; which, without it, will continually fly out of their proper orbits, and destroy the order and harmony of the political system."

"Mr. WILSON. — A discretion must be left on one side or the other. Will it not be most safely lodged on the side of the National Government?

Among the first sentiments expressed in the first Congress, one was, — that Virginia is no more, that Massachusetts is no more, that Pennsylvania is no more, etc.; we are now one Nation of brethren: we must bury all local interests and distinctions. This language continued for some time. . . . No sooner were the State Governments formed, than their jealousy and ambition began to display themselves. Each endeavored to cut a slice from the common loaf; . . till, at length, the Confederation became frittered down to the impotent condition in which it now stands. . . . To correct its vices is the business of this Convention. . . . What danger is there, that the whole will unnecessarily sacrifice a part? But, reverse the case, and leave the whole at the mercy of each part, and will not the general interest be continually sacrificed to local interests?"

" Mr. JOHN DICKINSON [from Delaware]. — We must take our choice of two things. We must either subject the States to the danger of being injured by the power of the National Government, or the latter to the danger of being injured by that of the States. He thought the danger greater from the States."

June 9th. — " Mr. BREARLY [of New Jersey]. — He was sorry, he said, that any question on this point [the rule of suffrage] was brought into view. It had been much agitated in Congress at the time of forming the Confederation, and was then rightly settled, by allowing each sovereign State an equal vote. Otherwise, the smaller States must have been destroyed, instead of being saved. . . . He had come to the Convention with a view of being as useful as he could, in giving energy and stability to the Federal Government. When the proposition for destroying the equality of votes came forward, he was astonished, he was alarmed. Is it fair, then, it will be asked, that Georgia should have an equal vote with Virginia? He would not say it was. What remedy, then? One only; that a map of the United States be spread out, that all the existing boundaries be erased, and that a new partition of the whole be made into thirteen equal parts."

" Mr. PATTERSON [of New Jersey] considered the proposition for a proportional representation as striking at the existence of the lesser States. . . . We have no power to go beyond the Federal scheme; and if we had, the people are not ripe for any other. We must follow the people; the people will not follow us. The proposition could not be maintained. . . . If we are to be considered as a Nation, all State distinctions must be abolished. The whole must be thrown into hotchpotch, and when an equal division is made, then there may be fairly an equality of representation. . . . . New Jersey will never confederate on the plan before the Committee; she would be swallowed up. He would rather submit to a monarch, to a despot, than to such a fate. He would not only oppose the plan here, but, on his return home, do everything in his power to defeat it there."

" Mr. WILSON. — As all authority was derived from the people, equal numbers of people ought to have an equal number of representatives; and different numbers of people, different numbers of representatives. This principle had been improperly violated in the Confederation, owing to the urgent circumstances of the time. . . . Representatives of different districts ought clearly to hold the same proportion to each other, as their respective constituents hold to each other. . . . A new partition of the States is desirable, but evidently and totally impracticable."

" Mr. WILLIAMSON [of North Carolina] illustrated the case by a comparison of the different States to counties of different sizes within the same State."

June 11th. — " Mr. RANDOLPH. — The National authority needs every support we can give it. . . . The Executive and Judiciary of the States, . . unless they be brought under some tie to the National system, will always lean too much to the State systems, whenever a contest arises between the two."

June 12th. — " MR. MADISON. — No member of the Convention could say what the opinions of his constituents were at this time. . . . We ought to consider what was right and necessary in itself for the attainment of a proper government. A plan adjusted to this idea will commend itself."

In another speech, on the same day, MR. MADISON said : —

" What we wished was, to give to the Government that stability which was everywhere called for. . . He conceived it to be of great importance that a stable and firm government, organized in the republican form, should be held out to the people. If this be not done, . . it is much to be feared, the time is not distant, when, in universal disgust, they will renounce the blessing which they have purchased at so dear a rate, and be ready for any change that may be proposed to them."

June 13th. — The Resolutions proposed by GOVERNOR RANDOLPH, having been taken up and acted on, the Committee rose, and MR. GORHAM made a Report, consisting of nineteen Resolutions ; the first of which was the following : —

" *Resolved*, That it is the opinion of this Committee, that a National Government ought to be established, consisting of a Supreme Legislative, Executive, and Judiciary."

They had accomplished so much in about two weeks, and were thus encouraged to anticipate a speedy, successful result of their efforts, in accordance with this Resolution.

The consideration of the Report was postponed till the next day, " to give opportunity for other plans to be proposed."

June 15th. — " MR. PATTERSON laid before the Convention the plan [only another edition of the Confederation, a little enlarged,] which, he said, several of the Deputations wished to be substituted in place of that proposed by MR. RANDOLPH."

The introduction of this plan changed the aspect of affairs essentially ; but it was agreed to refer it, together with the plan of MR. RANDOLPH, to a Committee of the Whole.

June 16th. — " *In Committee of the Whole,* on the Resolutions proposed by MR. PATTERSON and MR. RANDOLPH, —

" MR. LANSING [from New York] called for the reading of the first Resolution of each plan, which he considered as involving principles directly in contrast. That of MR. PATTERSON, says he, sustains the sovereignty of the respective States ; that of MR. RANDOLPH destroys it . . The plan of MR. RANDOLPH, in short, absorbs all power, except what may be exercised in the little local matters of the States, which are not objects worthy of the supreme cognizance. He grounds his preference of MR. PATTERSON's plan chiefly on two objections to that of MR. RANDOLPH, — first, want of power in the Convention to discuss and propose it ; secondly, the improbability of its being adopted."

" MR. PATTERSON said, as he had on a former occasion given his sentiments on the plan proposed by MR. RANDOLPH, he would now give his reasons in favor of that proposed by himself. He preferred it, because it accorded, — first, with the powers of the Convention ; secondly, with the sentiments of the people. . . I came here, not to speak my own sentiments, but the sentiments of those who sent me. Our object is not such a Government as may be best in itself, but such a Government as our constituents have authorized us to prepare, and as they will approve. . . .

If the sovereignty of the States is to be maintained, the representatives must be drawn immediately from the States, not from the people; and we have no power to vary the idea of equal sovereignty. The only expedient that will cure the difficulty is that of throwing the States into hotchpotch."

"Mr. Wilson entered into a contrast of the principal points of the two plans. . . . . With regard to the *power of the Convention*, he conceived himself authorized *to conclude nothing*, but to be at liberty *to propose anything*. . . With *regard to the sentiments of the people*, he conceived it difficult to know precisely what they are. . He could not persuade himself that the State Governments and sovereignties were so much the idols of the people, nor a National Government so obnoxious to them, as some supposed. Where do the people look, at present, for relief from the evils of which they complain? Is it from an internal reform in their Governments? No, sir. It is from the National councils that relief is expected. For these reasons, he did not fear that the people would not follow us into a National Government; and it will be a further recommendation of Mr. Randolph's plan, that it is to be submitted *to them*, and *not to the Legislatures*, for ratification."

"Mr. C. Pinckney. — He thought the Convention authorized to go any length, in recommending, which they found necessary to remedy the evils which produced this Convention."

"Mr. Randolph was not scrupulous on the point of power. When the salvation of the Republic was at stake, it would be treason to our trust, not to propose what we found necessary. . . . The true question is, whether we shall adhere to the Federal plan, or introduce the National plan. The insufficiency of the former has been fully displayed by the trial already made. There are but two modes by which the end of a General Government can be attained: the first, by coercion, as proposed by Mr. Patterson's plan; the second, by real legislation, as proposed by the other plan. Coercion, he pronounced to be *impracticable, expensive, cruel to individuals*. . . . We must resort, therefore, to a *national legislation over individuals;* for which Congress are unfit. . . . . They are a mere diplomatic body, and are always obsequious to the views of the States, who are always encroaching on the authority of the United States. A provision for harmony among the States — as in trade, naturalization, etc.; for crushing rebellion, whenever it may rear its crest; and for certain other general benefits — must be made. . . . . A National Government alone, properly constituted, will answer the purpose; and he begged it to be considered, that the present is the last moment for establishing one. After this select experiment, the people will yield to despair."

June 18th. —" Colonel Hamilton [from New York]. — He had been hitherto silent on the business before the Convention, partly from respect to others whose superior abilities, age, and experience, rendered him unwilling to bring forward ideas dissimilar to theirs, and partly from his delicate situation with respect to his own State, to whose sentiments, as expressed by his colleagues [Mr. Yates and Mr. Lansing], he could by no means accede. . The crisis, however, which now marked our affairs, was too serious to permit any scruples whatever to prevail over the duty imposed on every man to contribute his efforts for the public safety and happiness. As to the powers of the Convention, he thought the doubts started on that subject had arisen from distinctions and reasonings too subtle. . . . He agreed with the honorable gentleman from Virginia, Mr. Randolph, that we owed it to our country, to do in this emergency, whatever we should deem essential to its happiness. To rely on and propose any plan not adequate to its exigencies, merely because it was not clearly within our powers, would be to sacrifice the means to the end . . . . . The great question is, what provision shall we make for the happiness of our country? . . . The great and essential principles necessary for the support of government are, — first, an active and constant interest in supporting it. This principle does not exist in the States in favor of the Federal Government. They have evidently in a high degree, the *esprit de corps*. They constantly pursue internal interests adverse to those of the whole. They have their particular debts, their particular plans of finance, etc. All these, when opposed to, invariably prevail over, . . . the plans of Congress. . . The ambition of their demagogues is known to hate the control of the General Government.

. . . .

An habitual attachment of the people. The whole force of this tie is on the side of the State Government. . . . . . All the passions . . of avarice, ambition, interest, which govern most individuals, and all public bodies, fall into the current of the States, and do not flow into the stream of the General Government. The former, therefore, will generally be an overmatch for the General Government; and render any Confederacy in its very nature precarious. Theory is, in this case, fully confirmed by experience [as in the Amphictyonic Council, the German Confederacy, the Swiss Cantons, etc.]. How, then, are all these evils to be avoided? Only by such a complete sovereignty in the General Government as will turn all the strong principles and passions above mentioned on its side. . . If States are to deliberate on the mode, they will deliberate on the object, of the supplies; and will grant or not grant, as they approve or disapprove of it. . . . Bad principles in a government, though slow, are sure in their operation, and will gradually destroy it. . . Two sovereignties cannot coexist within the same limits. It was once thought that the power of Congress was amply sufficient to secure the end of their institution. The error is now seen by every one. . . . One of the weak sides of republics was their being liable to foreign influence and corruption. Men of little character, acquiring great power, become easily the tools of intermeddling neighbors. . . . What is the inference from all these observations? That we ought to go as far, in order to attain stability and permanency, as republican principles will admit."

June 19th. — " MR. MADISON . . observed that violations of the Federal Articles had been numerous and notorious. . . . He stated the object of a proper plan to be two-fold, — first, to preserve the Union ; secondly, to provide a Government that will remedy the evils felt by the States, both in their united and individual capacities. Examine MR. PATTERSON's plan. . . . Will it prevent the violations of the law of nations, and of treaties which, if not prevented, must involve us in foreign wars? The tendency of the States to these violations has been manifested in sundry instances. . . . Will it prevent encroachments on the Federal authority? A tendency to such encroachments has been sufficiently exemplified among ourselves, as well as in every other confederated republic, ancient or modern. . . . If we recur to the examples of other confederacies, we shall find in all of them, the same tendency of the parts to encroach on the authority of the whole. . . . In developing the evils which vitiate the political system of the United States, it is proper to take into view those which prevail within the States individually, as well as those which affect them collectively ; since the former indirectly affect the whole, and there is great reason to believe that the pressure of them had a full share in the motives which produced the present Convention. . . . . The great difficulty lies in the affair of representation. . . . Their language was, that it would not be safe for Delaware to allow Virginia sixteen times as many votes [as Delaware]. The expedient proposed by them was, that all the States should be thrown into one mass, and a new partition be made into thirteen equal parts. . . The dissimilarities . . amounted to a prohibition of the attempt."

On the question, whether the Committee should rise, and MR. RANDOLPH'S propositions be reported without alteration, . . . as preferable to those of MR. PATTERSON, — seven States in the affirmative, three in the negative, one divided.

MR. RANDOLPH'S plan, as reported by the Committee, *June 13th*, being then before the House, and the first Resolution, —"That a National Government ought to be established," etc.,* — being taken up,—

"MR. WILSON observed that, by a National Government, he did not mean one that would swallow up the State Governments. . . . They were absolutely necessary for certain purposes which the former could not reach. All large Governments must be subdivided into lesser jurisdictions."

"COLONEL HAMILTON coincided with the proposition as it stood in the Report. . . . No boundary could be drawn between the National and State Legislatures; the former must therefore have indefinite authority. If it were limited at all, the rivalship of the States would gradually subvert it. Even, as corporations, the extent of some of them, as Virginia, Massachusetts, etc., would be formidable. As *States*, he thought they ought to be abolished; but he admitted the necessity of leaving in them subordinate jurisdictions."

"MR. KING. — The States were not sovereigns, in the sense contended for by some. They did not possess the peculiar features of sovereignty. . . Considering them as political beings, they were dumb; for they could not speak to any foreign sovereign whatever. They were deaf; for they could not hear any proposition from such sovereign. . . Congress can act alone, without the States. . . No act of the States can vary the situation, or prevent the judicial consequences. If the States, therefore, retained some portion of their sovereignty, they had certainly divested themselves of essential portions of it. If they formed a Confederacy in some respects, they formed a Nation in others. He doubted much the practicability of annihilating the States; but thought much of their power ought to be taken from them."

"MR. LUTHER MARTIN said † he considered that the separation from Great Britain placed the thirteen States in a state of nature towards each other; . . . that he could never accede to a plan that would introduce an inequality, and lay ten States at the mercy of Virginia, Massachusetts, and Pennsylvania."

"MR. WILSON could not admit the doctrine. . . He read the Declaration of Independence, . . . inferring that they were independent, *not individually*, but *unitedly*."

"COLONEL HAMILTON assented to the doctrine of MR. WILSON. He denied the doctrine, that the States were thrown into a state of nature. . . . The more close the union of the States, and the more complete the authority of the whole, the less opportunity will be allowed to the stronger States to oppress the weaker."

June 20th. — The second Resolution, — "That the National Legislature ought to consist of two branches," — being taken up, —

"MR. LANSING moved, instead of the second Resolution, that the powers of Legislation be vested in Congress. He observed that the true question was, whether the Convention would adhere to, or depart from, the foundation of the present Confederacy. . . . It could not be expected that those possessing sovereignty would ever voluntarily part with it. It was not to be expected from any one State, much less from thirteen. . . . He doubted whether any General Government, equally beneficial to all,

* See that Resolution, p. 18.
† Mr. Martin was from Maryland. He took his seat in the Convention, *June 9th*.

can be attained. That now under consideration. he is sure, must be utterly unattainable. . . . The system was too novel and complex. No man could foresee what its operation will be, either with respect to the General Government, or the State Governments. One or the other, it has been surmised, must absorb the whole."

"Colonel Mason [from Virginia] did not expect this point would have been reagitated. The essential differences between the two plans had been clearly stated. The principal objections against that of Mr. Randolph were the *want of power* and the *want of practicability*. There can be no weight in the first, as the *fiat* is not to be here, but in the people. . . . The *impracticability* of gaining the public concurrence, he thought, was still more groundless. . . . He meant not to throw any reflections on Congress, as a body, much less on any particular members of it. He meant, however, to speak his sentiments, without reserve, on this subject. . . . Is it to be thought that the people of America . . . will surrender both the sword and the purse to the same body,—and that, too, not chosen by themselves? . . . Will they give unbounded confidence to a secret journal,—to the intrigues, to the factions, which, in the nature of things, appertain to such an assembly? If any man doubts the existence of these characters of Congress, let him consult their journals for the years '78, '79, and '80. . . . It was acknowledged by Mr. Patterson that his plan could not be enforced without military coercion. Does he consider the force of this concession? . . . Rebellion is the only case in which the military force of the State can be properly exerted against its citizens. In one point of view, he was struck with horror at the prospect of recurring to this expedient. . . . He took this occasion to repeat, that, notwithstanding his solicitude to establish a National Government, he never would agree to abolish the State Governments, or render them absolutely insignificant. . . The Convention . . could not be expected to make a faultless Government. And he should prefer trusting to posterity the amendment of its defects, rather than to push the experiment too far."

"Mr. Luther Martin agreed with Colonel Mason, as to the importance of the State Governments. He would support them, at the expense of the General Government, which was instituted for the purpose of that support. He saw no necessity for two branches; and, if it existed, Congress might be organized into two. . . . . He thought . . that a National Judiciary, extended into the States, would be ineffectual, and would be viewed with a jealousy inconsistent with its usefulness."

"Mr. Sherman [from Connecticut] seconded and supported Mr. Lansing's motion. . . Congress carried us through the war; and, perhaps, as well as any government would have done. . . . All the States were sensible of the defect of power in Congress. He thought much might be said in apology for the failure of the State Legislatures to comply with the Confederation. . . · Congress, indeed, by the Confederation, have, in fact, the right of saying how much the people shall pay, and to what purpose it shall be applied: and this right was granted to them in the expectation that it would in all cases have its effect."

"Mr. Wilson urged the necessity of two branches. . . [After noticing the defects of other Confederacies], he appealed to our own experience of the defects of our own Confederacy. He had been, six years of the twelve since the commencement of the Revolution, a member of Congress, and had felt all its weaknesses. . . The success of the Revolution was owing to other causes than the constitution of Congress. In many instances, it went even against the difficulties arising from Congress themselves. He insisted that a jealousy would exist between the State Legislatures and the General Legislature; observing that the members of the former would have views and feelings very distinct, in this respect, from their constituents. . . . He observed that the addresses of Congress to the people at large had always been better received, and produced greater effect, than those made to the Legislatures.''

The question was then taken ; and MR. LANSING'S motion, seconded by MR. SHERMAN, was lost, — *Aye*, four ; *No*, six.

June 21st. — The second Resolution in the Report of the Committee of the Whole, — "That the National Legislature ought to consist of two branches," — being again under consideration, —

"MR. WILSON. — It was asked, how the General Government and individuality of the particular States could be reconciled to each other, and how the latter could be secured against the former? Might it not, on the other side, be asked, how the former was to be secured against the latter? . . . The General Government will be as ready to preserve the rights of the States as the latter are to preserve the rights of individuals, all the members of the former having a common interest, as representatives of all the people of the latter, to leave the State Governments in possession of what the people wish them to retain. He could not discover, therefore, any danger whatever on the side from which it was apprehended. On the contrary, he conceived that, in spite of every precaution, the General Government would be in perpetual danger of encroachments from the State Governments.''

" MR. MADISON was of opinion, in the first place, that there was less danger of encroachment from the General Government than from the State Governments ; and, in the second place, that the mischiefs from encroachments would be less fatal, if made by the former than if made by the latter.

"All the examples of other confederacies prove the greater tendency, in such systems, to anarchy than to tyranny ; to disobedience of the members than to usurpations of the federal head. Our own experience had fully illustrated this tendency. . . . In some of the States, particularly in Connecticut, all the townships are incorporated, and have certain limited jurisdictions. Have the representatives of the people of the townships, in the Legislature of the State, ever endeavored to despoil the townships of any part of their local authority? . . . . The relation of a General Government to State Governments is parallel.

" Guards were more necessary against the encroachments of the State Governments on the General Government, than of the latter on the former. . . . . Were it practicable for the General Government to extend its care to every requisite object, without the cooperation of the State Governments, the people would not be less free, as members of one great Republic than as members of thirteen small ones. . . . Supposing, therefore, a tendency in the General Government to absorb the State Governments, no *fatal* consequences could result. Taking the reverse as the supposition, that a tendency should be left in the State Governments towards an independence on the General Government, and the gloomy consequences need not be pointed out. The imagination of them must have suggested to the States the experiment we are now making to prevent the calamity, and must have formed the chief motive with those present to undertake the arduous task.''

The question being taken on the Resolution, — " That the Legislature ought to consist of two branches," — the votes were, *Aye*, seven ; *No*, three. Maryland divided, and therefore not counted.

The third Resolution of the Report, on the 13th, — " That the members of the first branch of the National Legislature ought to be elected by the people of the several States," — being taken up, —

" GENERAL PINCKNEY [from South Carolina] moved that the first branch, instead of being elected by the people, should be elected in such manner as the Legislature of each State should direct."

" MR. L. MARTIN seconded the motion."

" COLONEL HAMILTON considered the motion as intended manifestly to transfer the election from the people to the State Legislatures, which would essantially vitiate the plan. It would increase the State influence, which could not be too watchfully guarded against."

" MR. SHERMAN would like an election by the Legislatures best, but is content with the plan as it stands."

" MR. WILSON considered the election of the first branch by the people not only as the corner-stone, but as the foundation of the fabric. . . . The Legislatures are actuated not merely by the sentiment of the people, but have an official sentiment opposed to that of the General Government, and perhaps to that of the people themselves."

" MR. KING enlarged on the same distinction."

"On the question for GENERAL PINCKNEY's motion, *Aye*, four; *No*, six ; Maryland, divided."

" On the question for the election of the first branch by the people, *Aye*, nine ; *No*, one; Maryland, divided."

June 22d. — The clause in the third Resolution, — "To receive fixed stipends . . out of the National Treasury," — being considered, —

" MR. ELLSWORTH [from Connecticut] moved to substitute payment by the States out of their own treasuries."

" MR. GORHAM wished not to refer the matter to the State Legislatures. . . . Let the National Legislature provide for their own wages, from time to time, as the State Legislatures do."

" MR. RANDOLPH. — If the States were to pay the members of the National Legislature, a dependence would be created that would vitiate the whole system. The whole nation has an interest in the attendance and services of the members. The National Treasury, therefore, is the proper fund for supporting them."

" MR. KING urged the danger of creating a dependence on the States, by leaving to them the payment of the members of the National Legislature."

" MR. SHERMAN contended for referring both the quantum and the payment of it to the State Legislatures."

" MR. WILSON. — He thought it of great moment, that the members of the National Government should be left as independent as possible of the State Governments in all respects."

" MR. MADISON concurred in the necessity of preserving the compensations for the National Government independent of the State Governments."

" COLONEL HAMILTON. — He was strenuous against making the National Council dependent on the legislative rewards of the States. . . . He expatiated emphatically on the difference between the feelings and views of the *people* and those of the *Government* of the States, arising from the personal interests and official inducements which must render the latter unfriendly to the General Government."

On the question for striking out "National Treasury," as moved by MR. ELLSWORTH. —

"COLONEL HAMILTON renewed his opposition to it. He pressed the distinction between *the State Governments* and *the people*. The former would be the rivals of the General Government. The State Legislatures ought not, therefore, to be paymasters of the latter."

On the question for MR. ELLSWORTH'S motion, *Aye*, four; *No*, five.

June 25th. — The Resolution in the Report, — "That the members of the second branch of the National Legislature ought to be chosen by the individual Legislatures," — being taken up, —

"MR. CHARLES PINCKNEY. — The efficacy of the system will depend on this Article. In order to form a right judgment in the case, it will be proper to examine the situation of this country. . . . . .

"Our true situation appears to me to be this, — a new, extensive country, containing within itself the materials for forming a Government capable of extending to its citizens all the blessings of civil and religious liberty ; capable of making them happy at home. This is the great end of republican establishments. . . . The people of the United States may be divided into three classes, — professional men, . . . commercial men, . . and the landed interest, the owners and cultivators of the soil. . . . . These three classes, however distinct in their pursuits, are individually equal in the political scale, and may be easily proved to have but one interest. The dependence of each on the other is mutual. The merchant depends on the planter. Both must, in private as well as public affairs, be connected with the professional men ; who, in their turn, must in some measure depend on them. Hence it is clear, . . that, after all, there is one, but one, great and equal body of citizens composing the inhabitants of this country. . . For a people thus circumstanced are we, then, to form a Government ; and the question is, what sort of Government is best suited to them ? . . We must, as has been observed, suit our Government to the people it is to direct. These are, I believe, as active, intelligent, and as susceptible of good government as any people in the world. The confusion which has produced the present relaxed state is not owing to them. It is owing to the weakness and defects of a Government incapable of combining the various interests it is intended to unite, and destitute of energy. All that we have to do, then, is to distribute the powers of government in such a manner, and for such limited periods, as, while it gives a proper degree of permanency to the magistrate, will reserve to the people the right of election, which they will not or ought not frequently to part with. I am of opinion, that this may easily be done ; and that, with some amendments, the propositions before the Committee will fully answer this end."

"MR. WILSON. — . . . It was necessary to observe the two-fold relation in which the people will stand, first, as citizens of the General Government ; and, secondly, as citizens of their particular State. The General Government was meant for them, in the first capacity ; the State Governments, in the second. Both Governments were derived from the people ; both meant for the people ; both, therefore, ought to be regulated on the same principles. The same train of ideas which belonged to the relation of the citizens to their State Governments were applicable to their relations to the General Government. And, in forming the latter, we ought to proceed by abstracting as much as possible from the idea of the State Governments. . . The General Government is not an Assemblage of States, but of individuals, for certain political purposes ; it is not meant for the States, but for the individuals composing them ; the individuals, therefore, not the States, ought to be represented in it."

On the question to agree " That the members of the second branch be chosen by the individual Legislatures," *Aye,* nine ; *No,* two.

The clause, — " That the second branch hold their offices for a term of seven years," — being considered, —

" Mr. READ proposed that they should hold their offices during good behavior."

" Mr. ROBERT MORRIS [from Pennsylvania] seconds him." *

June 26th. — The duration of the second branch being again under consideration, —

" Mr. GORHAM moved to fill the blank with six years, one-third of the members to go out every second year."

" Mr. WILSON seconded the motion."

" GENERAL PINCKNEY opposed six, in favor of four years."

" Mr. READ moved that the term be nine years. . . He would still prefer ' during good behavior ;' but, being little supported in that idea, he was willing to take the longest term that could be obtained."

" Mr. JACOB BROOM [from Delaware] seconded the motion."

" Mr. MADISON. — In order to judge of the form to be given to this institution, it would be proper to take a view of the ends to be served by it. These were, — first, to protect the people against their rulers ; secondly, to protect the people against the transient impressions into which they themselves might be led. . . Such being the objects of the second branch in the proposed Government, he thought a considerable duration ought to be given to it. He did not conceive that the term of nine years could threaten any real danger. . . . He observed that, as it was more than probable we were now digesting a plan, which, in its operation, would decide forever the fate of republican government, we ought not only to provide every guard to liberty that its preservation could require, but be equally careful to supply the defects which our own experience had particularly pointed out."

" Mr. READ wished it to be considered by the small States that it was their interest that we should become one people as much as possible ; that State attachments should be extinguished as much as possible ; that the Senate should be so constituted as to have the feelings of citizens of the whole."

" COLONEL HAMILTON. — He did not mean to enter particularly into the subject. He concurred with Mr. MADISON in thinking we were now to decide forever the fate of republican government ; and if we did not give to that form due stability and wisdom, it would be disgraced and lost among ourselves, disgraced and lost to mankind forever. . . He concurred, also, in the general observations of Mr. MADISON on the subject, which might be supported by others, if it were necessary. It was certainly true that nothing like an equality of property existed ; that an inequality would exist as long as liberty existed, and that it would result from that very liberty itself."

" Mr. GERRY wished we could be united in our ideas concerning a permanent Government. All aim at the same end; but there are great differences as to the means. . . The Convention ought to be extremely cautious in what they hold out to the people. . . . If the plan should

---

* In a generally approved history of the Revolution, it is stated that the pecuniary services of Robert Morris contributed hardly less to the success of that wonderful struggle, than did the military services of General Washington.

be of such a nature as to rouse a violent opposition, it is easy to foresee that discord and confusion will ensue. . . . He admitted the evils arising from a frequency of elections, and would agree to give the Senate a duration of four or five years A longer term would defeat itself. It never would be adopted by the people."

" Mr. Wilson. — . . . . The true reason why Great Britain has not yet listened to a commercial treaty with us has been, because she has no confidence in the stability or efficacy of our Government. Nine years, with a rotation, will provide these desirable qualities. . . In such a body, the personal character will be lost in the political. The popular objection against appointing any public body for a long term was that it might, by gradual encroachments, prolong itself, first, into a body for life, and finally become a hereditary one. . . . As one-third would go out triennially, there would be always three divisions, holding their places for unequal terms, and consequently acting under the influence of different views and different impulses."

On the question for nine years, *Aye*, three ; *No*, eight.

On the question for six years, *Aye*, seven ; *No*, four.

The clause of the fourth Resolution, — " To receive a compensation for their services," — being under consideration, —

" Mr. Ellsworth moved to strike out ' to be paid out of the National Treasury,' and insert ' to be paid by their respective States.' "

" Mr. Madison considered this as a departure from a fundamental principle, and subverting the end intended, by allowing the Senate a duration of six years. . . . The motion would make the Senate, like Congress, the mere agents and advocates of State interests and views, instead of being the impartial umpires and guardians of justice and the general good."

" Mr. Jonathan Dayton [from New Jersey] considered the payment of the Senate by the States as fatal to their independence. He was decided for paying them out of the National Treasury." *

On the question for payment of the Senate, as moved by Mr. Ellsworth, *Aye*, five ; *No*, six.

On the question, whether the words " to be paid out of the National Treasury " should stand, *Aye*, five ; *No*, six.

June 27th. — A question being proposed on the Resolution declaring " that the suffrage in the first branch should be according to an equitable ratio " [of representation], — .

" Mr. Luther Martin contended, at great length, and with great eagerness, that the General Government was meant merely to preserve the State Governments, not to govern individuals ; that its powers ought to be kept within narrow limits . . . That individuals, as such, have little to do but with their own States. . . . That the States, like individuals, were in a state of nature, equally sovereign and free. . . . That the propositions on the table were a system of slavery for ten States. . . . That it will be in vain to propose any plan offensive to the rulers of the States, whose influence over the people will certainly prevent their adopting it "

June 28th. — " Mr. Madison said he was much disposed to concur in any expedient, not inconsistent with fundamental principles, that

* Mr. Dayton took his seat in the Convention, *June 21st.*

could remove the difficulty concerning the rule of representation. But he could neither be convinced that the rule contended for was just, nor that it was necessary for the safety of the small States against the large States. That it was not just, had been conceded by Mr. BREARLY and Mr. PATTERSON themselves. The expedient proposed by them was a new partition of the territory of the United States. . . . . . The true policy of the small States lies in promoting those principles, and that form of Government, which will most approximate the States to the condition of counties. . . . Give to the General Government sufficient energy and permanency, and gradual partitions of the large, and junctions of the small, States will be facilitated; and time may effect that equalization which is wished for by the small States now, but can never be accomplished at once."

"DOCTOR [BENJAMIN] FRANKLIN. — Mr. President, the small progress we have made, after four or five weeks' close attendance and continual reasonings with each other, . . is, methinks, a melancholy proof of the imperfection of the human understanding. . . We have gone back to ancient history for models of government, . . and we have viewed modern States all round Europe, but find none of their Constitutions suitable to our circumstances. . . In the beginning of the contest with Great Britain, when we were sensible of danger, we had daily prayers in this room for the Divine protection. . . . All of us, who were engaged in the struggle, must have observed frequent instances of a superintending Providence in our favor. To that kind Providence we owe this happy opportunity of considering, in peace, on the means of establishing our future National felicity. . . . I have lived, sir, a long time; and the longer I live, the more convincing proofs I see of this truth, — that God governs in the affairs of men. . . . I firmly believe this; and I also believe, that without His concurring aid, we shall succeed in this political building no better than the builders of Babel. We shall be divided by our little partial local interests ; our projects will be confounded ; and we ourselves shall become a reproach and byword down to future ages. . . . . . . "I therefore beg leave to move, that henceforth, prayers, imploring the Divine assistance of Heaven, and its blessings on our deliberations, be held in this Assembly, every morning, before we proceed to business."

The following is Mr. MADISON'S explanation of the manner in which this address was received and disposed of in the Convention : —

"Mr. SHERMAN seconded the motion."

"COLONEL HAMILTON and several others expressed their apprehensions, that, however proper such a Resolution might have been at the beginning of the Convention, it might, at this late day, in the first place, bring on it some disagreeable animadversions [because so long omitted] ; and, in the second, lead the public to believe that the embarrassments and dissensions within the Convention had suggested this measure."

"Mr. WILLIAMSON observed that the true cause of the omission could not be mistaken. The Convention had no funds."

"Mr. RANDOLPH proposed, in order to give a favorable aspect to the measure, that a sermon be preached, at the request of the Convention, on the Fourth of July, the anniversary of Independence ; and thenceforward, prayers, etc., be read in the Convention every morning."

"DOCTOR FRANKLIN seconded this motion."

"After several unsuccessful attempts for silently postponing this matter by adjourning, the adjournment was at length carried, without any vote on the motion."

June 29th. — " DOCTOR JOHNSON [from Connecticut]. — The controversy must be endless whilst gentlemen differ in the grounds of their arguments ; those on one side considering the States as districts of people composing one political society, those on the other considering them as so many political societies. . . . . . . On the whole, he thought that, as in some respects, the States are to be considered in their political capacity, and in others as districts of individual citizens, the two ideas embraced on different sides, instead of being opposed to each other, ought to be combined ; that in one branch, the people ought to be represented ; in the other, the States."

" MR. GORHAM. — He conceived that a rupture of the Union would be an event unhappy for all ; but surely the large States would be least unable to take care of themselves. . . . On the whole, he considered a union of the States as necessary to their happiness, and a firm General Government as necessary to their union. He should consider it his duty, if his colleagues viewed the matter in the same light he did, to stay here as long as any other State would remain with them, in order to agree on some plan that could, with propriety, be recommended to the people."

" MR. ELLSWORTH did not despair. He still trusted that some good plan of Government would be devised and adopted."

" MR. READ. — He should have no objection to the system if it were truly *national*, but it has too much of a *federal* mixture in it. . . . . Delaware had enjoyed tranquillity, and, he flattered himself, would continue to do so. He was not, however, so selfish as not to wish for a good General Government. In order to obtain one, the whole States must be incorporated. . . They must be done away. The ungranted lands, also, which have been assumed by particular States, must be given up. He repeated his approbation of the plan of MR. HAMILTON, and wished it to be substituted for that on the table."

" MR. MADISON agreed with DOCTOR JOHNSON, that the mixed nature of the Government ought to be kept in view, but thought too much stress was laid on the rank of States as political societies. . . He pointed out the limitations on the sovereignty of the States, as now confederated. . . He entreated the gentlemen representing the small States to renounce a principle which was confessedly unjust ; which could never be admitted ; and which, if admitted, must infuse mortality into a Constitution which we wished to last forever. He prayed them to ponder well the consequences of suffering the Confederacy to go to pieces. . . . The same causes which have rendered the Old World the theatre of incessant wars, and have banished liberty from the face of it, would soon produce the same effects here. . . . . These consequences, he conceived, ought to be apprehended ; whether the States should run into a total separation from each other, or should enter into partial confederacies. Either event would be truly deplorable ; and those who might be accessory to either could never be forgiven by their country, nor by themselves." •

" COLONEL HAMILTON observed that individuals forming political societies modify their rights differently, with regard to suffrage. Examples of it are found in all the States. . . . But, as States are a collection of individual men, which ought we to respect most, the rights of the people composing them, or of the artificial beings resulting from the composition ? Nothing could be more preposterous and absurd than to sacrifice the former to the latter. It has been said, that if the smaller States renounce their equality, they renounce at the same time their liberty. The truth is, it is a contest for power, not for liberty. Will the men composing the small States be less free than those composing the larger ? . . . Will the people of Delaware be less free, if each citizen have an equal vote with each citizen of Pennsylvania ? . . . No considerable inconveniences had been found from the division of the State of New York into districts of different sizes. Some of the consequences of a dissolution of the Union, and of the establishment of partial confederacies, have been pointed out. He would add another, of a most serious nature. Alliances . . with different and hostile nations of Europe, who will make us parties to all their own quarrels. . . It has been said, that respectability in the eyes of foreign nations was not the object at which we aimed; that the proper object of republican government was domestic tranquillity and happiness. . . No government could give us tranquillity and happiness at home, which did not possess sufficient stability and strength to make us respected abroad. This was the critical moment for forming such a government. . . As yet, we retain the habits of union. We are weak, and sensible of our weakness. Henceforward, the motives will become feebler and the difficulties greater. It is a miracle that we are now here, exercising our tranquil and free deliberations on the subject. It would be madness to trust to future miracles. A thousand causes must obstruct a reproduction of them." *

"Mr. WILLIAM PIERCE [from Georgia]. — The members of Congress were advocates for local advantages. State distinctions must be sacrificed, as far as the general good required, but without destroying the States. Though from a small State, he felt himself a citizen of the United States, whose general interest he would always support." †

"Mr. GERRY urged that we never were independent States, were not such now, and never could be, even on the principle of the Confederation. . . . The present Confederation he considered as dissolving. The fate of the Union will be decided by the Convention."

"Mr LUTHER MARTIN remarked, that the language of States being sovereign and independent, was once familiar and understood, though it seemed now so strange and obscure."

"Mr. ELLSWORTH. — To the eastward, he was sure Massachusetts was the only State that would listen to a proposition for excluding the States, as equal political societies, from an equal voice in both branches. The others would risk every consequence, rather than part with so dear a right."

June 30th. — "Mr. WILSON. — The gentleman from Connecticut (Mr. ELLSWORTH) had pronounced that, if the motion [for an equal vote in the second branch] should not be acceded to, of all the States north of Pennsylvania, one only would agree to any General Government. . . . He hoped the alarms exceeded their cause, and that they would not abandon a country to which they were bound by so many strong and endearing ties. . . Can we forget for whom we are forming a Government? Is it for *men*, or for the imaginary beings called *States?* . . . It is all a mere illusion of names. We talk of States till we forget what they are composed of. . . Bad governments are of two sorts, — first, that which does too little; secondly, that which does too much, — that which fails through weakness, and that which destroys through oppression. Under which of these evils do the United States at present groan? Under the weakness and inefficiency of its Government. To remedy this weakness, we have been sent to this Convention."

"Mr. MADISON. — He contended that the States were divided into different interests, not by their difference of size, but by other circumstances; the most natural of which resulted partly from climate, but principally from the effects of their having or not having slaves. These two causes concurred in forming the great division of the interests in the United States. It did not lie between the large and small States. It lay

---

* From that day, Colonel Hamilton was absent till *August* 13th.
† A few of these extracts are taken from Judge Yates's Journal. Mr. Pierce took his seat in the Convention, *May* 31st.

between the Northern and Southern; and, if any defensive power were necessary, it ought to be mutually given to those two interests."

" Mr. ELLSWORTH assured the House that, whatever might be thought of the Representatives of Connecticut, the State was entirely Federal in her disposition."

" Mr. SHERMAN. — Congress is not to blame for the faults of the States. Their measures have been right, and the only thing wanting has been a further power in Congress to render them effectual."

" Mr. WILLIAM R. DAVIE [from North Carolina] was much embarrassed. If a proportional representation was attended with insuperable difficulties, the making the Senate the representative of the States [as moved by Mr. ELLSWORTH] looked like bringing us back to Congress again, and shutting out all the advantages expected from it." *

" Mr KING observed, . . that a reform would be nugatory and nominal only, if we should make another Congress of the proposed Senate; that if the adherence to an equality of votes was fixed and unalterable, there could not be less obstinacy on the other side. . . That he was, however, filled with astonishment, that, if we were convinced that every man in America was secure in all his rights, we should be ready to sacrifice this substantial good to the phantom of State Sovereignty.   That his feelings were more harrowed, and his fears more agitated, for his country, than he could express; that he conceived this to be the last opportunity of providing for its liberty and happiness; that he could not, therefore but repeat his amazemement, that, when a just Government, founded on a fair representation of the people of America, was within our reach, we should renounce the blessing, from an attachment to the ideal freedom and importance of States.   That, should this wonderful illusion continue to prevail, his mind was prepared for every event, rather than sit down under a Government founded on a vicious principle of representation, and which must be as short-lived as it would be unjust."

" Mr. DAYTON. — It should have been shown, that the evils we have experienced have proceeded from the equality now objected to; and that the seeds of dissolution for the State Governments are not sown in the General Government."

" Mr. MARTIN would not confederate, if it could not be done on just principles."

" Mr. MADISON. — The plan, in its present shape, makes the Senate absolutely dependent on the States.   The Senate, therefore, is only another edition of Congress.   He knew the faults of that body, and had used a bold language against it."

" Mr. GUNNING BEDFORD [from Delaware] contended that there was no middle ground between a perfect consolidation, and a mere confederacy, of the States.   The first is out of the question; and in the latter they must continue, if not perfectly, yet equally, sovereign. . .   The three large States have a common interest to bind them together in commerce.   But, whether a combination, as we supposed, or a competition, as others supposed, should take place among them, — in either case, the small States will be ruined.   We must, like Solon, make such a Government as the people will approve. . . .   It is not true that the people will not agree to enlarge the powers of the present Congress. The language of the people has been, that Congress ought to have the power of collecting the impost, and of coercing the States where it may be necessary. . .   We have been told, . . that this is the last moment for a fair trial in favor of a good Government. It will be the last, indeed, if the propositions reported from the Committee go forth to the people.   He was under no apprehensions.   The large States

* Mr. Davie took his seat at the opening of the Convention.

dare not dissolve the Confederation. If they do, the small ones will find some foreign ally, of more honor and good faith, who will take them by the hand, and do them justice. He did not mean by this to intimidate or alarm. It was a natural consequence, which ought to be avoided by enlarging the Federal powers, not by annihilating the Federal system. This is what the people expect. All agree in the necessity of a more efficient Government, and why not make such an one as they desire ? " *

"Mr. Ellsworth. — Under a National Government, he should participate in the national security, as remarked by Mr. King ; but that was all. What he wanted was domestic happiness."

"Mr. King was for preserving the States in·a subordinate degree, and as far as they would be necessary for the purposes stated by Mr. Ellsworth. . . . For himself, whatever might be his distress, he never would court relief from a foreign power."

July 2d. — "Mr. C. Pinckney. — . . He was extremely anxious that something should be done, considering this as the last appeal to a regular experiment. Congress have failed in almost every effort for an amendment of the Federal system. Nothing has prevented a dissolution of it but the appointment of this Convention ; and he could not express his alarms for the consequence of such an event."

"General Pinckney. — . . Some compromise seemed to be necessary, the States being equally divided on the question for an equality of votes in the second branch. He proposed that a Committee, consisting of a member from each State, should be appointed to devise and report some compromise."

"Mr. L. Martin had no objection to a commitment ; but no modifications whatever could reconcile the smaller States to the least diminution of their equal sovereignty."

"Mr. Sherman. — We are now at a full stop. . . A Committee he thought most likely to hit on some expedient."

"Mr. Gouverneur Morris [a delegate from Pennsylvania] thought a Committee advisable, as the Convention had been equally divided." †

"Mr. Randolph favored a commitment, though he did not expect much benefit from the expedient."

"Mr. Caleb Strong [from Massachusetts] was for the commitment."

"Mr. Lansing would not oppose the commitment, though he expected little advantage from it."

How changed the prospect since the 13th of June ! ‡
This was indeed an appalling crisis in the business of the Convention. It was evidently so regarded by its members. A number of those members, however, doubtless anticipated or apprehended such kind of crisis, from the apparent determination evinced to procure, if possible, the substitution of the plan proposed by Mr. Patterson, on the 15*th* of *June,* § for the one proposed by Mr. Randolph, at the beginning.

"Mr. Williamson. — If we do not concede on both sides, our business will soon be at an end."

"Mr. Gerry was for the commitment. Something must be done, or we

* Mr. Bedford took his seat at the opening of the Convention.
† Mr. Morris was in the Convention at its opening, but left soon after the commencement of its business. Having been so long absent, he had now just returned from New York.
‡ See p. 18.   § See p. 18.

shall disappoint, not only America, but the whole world. . . Accommodation is absolutely necessary, and defects may be amended by a future Convention."

" Mr. Madison. — If you appoint one from each State, we shall have in it the whole force of State prejudices. The great difficulty is to conquer former opinions. The motion of the gentleman from South Carolina can be as well decided here as in committee."

The Committee was appointed by ballot. It consisted of " Mr. Gerry, Mr. Ellsworth, Mr. Yates, Mr. Patterson, Dr. Franklin, Mr. Bedford, Mr. Martin, Mr. Mason, Mr. Davie, Mr. Rutledge, Mr. Baldwin."

The Convention then adjourned to Thursday, *July 5th.*

July 5th. — "The Report of the Committee was read."

" That, in the first branch of the Legislature, each of the States now in the Union be allowed one member for every forty thousand inhabitants. . . That each State, not containing that number, shall be allowed one member.

" That all bills for raising or appropriating money, and for fixing the salaries of the officers of the government of the United States, shall originate in the first branch ; .. . and that no money shall be drawn from the public Treasury, but in pursuance of appropriations to be originated in the first branch.

" That, in the second branch of the Legislature, each State shall have an equal vote."

" Mr. Gorham. — I call for an explanation of the principles on which it [the Report] is grounded."

" Mr. Martin. — The one representation is proposed as an expedient for the adoption of the other."

" Mr. Wilson. — The Committee have exceeded their powers."

" Mr. Martin proposed to take the question on the whole of the Report."

" Mr. Wilson. — I do not choose to take a leap in the dark. I have a right to call for a division of the question on each distinct proposition."

" Mr Madison could not regard the privilege of originating money bills as any concession on the side of the small States. Experience proved that it had no effect. . . It was in vain to purchase concord in the Convention on terms which would perpetuate discord among their constituents. The Convention ought to pursue a plan which would bear the test of examination, which would be espoused and supported by the enlightened and impartial part of America ; and which they could themselves vindicate and urge. . . The merits of the system alone can finally and effectually obtain the public suffrage. He was not apprehensive that the people of the small States would obstinately refuse to accede to a Government founded on just principles, and promising them substantial protection. . . . . Harmony in the Convention was, no doubt, much to be desired. Satisfaction to all the States, in the first instance, still more so. But if the principal States, comprehending a majority of the people of the United States, should concur in a just and judicious plan, he had the firmest hopes that all the other States would by degrees accede to it."

" Mr. Gouverneur Morris. — . . He came here as a Representative of America ; he flattered himself he came here, in some degree, as a

Representative of the whole human race ; for the whole human race will be affected by the proceedings of this Convention. He wished gentlemen to extend their views beyond the present moment of time, beyond the narrow limits of place from which they derive their political origin. If he were to believe some things which he had heard, he should suppose that we were assembled to truck and bargain for our particular States. He cannot descend to think that any gentlemen are really actuated by these views. We must look forward to the effects of what we do. These alone ought to guide us. Much has been said of the sentiments of the people. They are unknown. They could not be known. All that we can infer, is, that if the plan we recommend be reasonable and right, all who have reasonable minds and sound-intentions will embrace it, notwithstanding what has been said by some gentlemen. Let us suppose that the larger States shall agree, and that the smaller refuse ; and let us trace the consequences. . . *This country must be united. If persuasion does not unite it, the sword will.* He begged this consideration might have its weight. The scenes of horror attending civil commotions cannot be described ; and the conclusion of them will be worse than the term of their continuance. . . State attachments and State importance have been the bane of this country. We cannot annihilate, but we may perhaps take out the teeth of, the serpents. He wished our ideas to be enlarged to the true interest of man, instead of being circumscribed within the narrow compass of a particular spot. And, after all, how little can be the motive yielded by selfishness for such a policy? Who can say whether he himself, much less whether his children, will the next year be an inhabitant of this or that State ? "

" Mr. BEDFORD. — . . No man can foresee to what extremities the small States may be driven by oppression. . . . The smaller States have conceded as to the constitution of the first branch, and as to money bills. If they be not gratified by correspondent concessions as to the second branch, is it to be supposed that they will ever accede to the plan? And what will be the consequence, if nothing should be done? The condition of the United States requires that something should be immediately done. It is better that a defective plan should be adopted, than that none should be recommended. He saw no reason why defects might not be supplied by meetings ten, fifteen, or twenty years hence."

" Mr. GERRY.— Though he had assented to the Report in the Committee, he had very material objections to it. We were, however, in a peculiar situation. We were neither the same nation, nor different nations. We ought not, therefore, to pursue the one or the other of these ideas too closely. If no compromise should take place, . . a secession, he foresaw, would take place ; for some gentlemen seemed decided on it. Two different plans would be proposed, and the result no man could foresee."

July 6th. — " Mr. GOUVERNEUR MORRIS moved to commit so much of the Report as relates to one member for every forty thousand inhabitants."

" Mr. WILSON seconded the motion, but with a view of leaving the Committee under no implied shackles."

" Mr. GORHAM apprehended great inconvenience from fixing directly the number of Representatives to be allowed to each State. He thought the number of inhabitants the true guide ; though perhaps some departure might be expedient from the full proportion."

" Mr. GERRY. — . . He favored the commitment, and thought that representation ought to be in the combined ratio of numbers of inhabitants and of wealth, and not of either singly."

" Mr. KING wished the clause to be committed, chiefly in order to detach it from the Report, with which it had no connection."

" MR. PINCKNEY saw no good reason for committing. The value of land had been found, on full investigation, to be an impracticable rule.* . . The number of inhabitants appeared to him the only just and practicable rule."

MR. MORRIS's motion prevailed; and the Committee was appointed, consisting of five members.

July 7th. — The question, — "Shall the clause allowing each State one vote in the second branch stand in the Report?" — being taken up, —

" MR. GERRY.— . . He had rather agree to it than have no accommodation. A Government. short of a proper national plan, if generally acceptable, would be preferable to a proper one which, if it could be carried at all, would operate on discontented States. He thought it would be best to suspend the question till the Committee appointed yesterday should make report."

" MR. SHERMAN supposed that it was the wish of every one that some General Government should be established."

" MR. WILSON was not deficient in a conciliatory temper; but, . . conciliation . . was pursued here rather among the Representatives, than among the constituents; and it would be of little consequence if not established among the latter. There could be little hope of its being established among them, if the foundation should not be laid in justice and right."

On the question, — " Shall the words stand as part of the Report?" — *Aye,* six; *No,* three.

" MR. PATTERSON would not decide whether the privilege concerning money bills were a valuable consideration, or not; but, . . after the establishment of that point [the rule of representation in the first branch], the small States would never be able to defend themselves without an equality of votes in the second branch. There was no other ground of accommodation. His resolution was fixed. He would meet the large States on that ground, and no other."

" MR. GOUVERNEUR MORRIS. — He had no resolution unalterably fixed, except to do what should finally appear to him right. He was against the Report, because it maintained the improper constitution of the second branch. It made it another Congress. . . It had been said by MR. GERRY, that the new Government would be partly National, partly Federal; that it ought, in the first quality, to protect individuals; in the second, the State. But, in what quality was it to protect the aggregate interest of the whole? . . It had been one of our greatest misfortunes, that the great objects of the Nation had been sacrificed constantly to local views. . . . We must have an efficient Government; and if there be an efficiency in the local [State] Governments, the former is impossible. . . He will be ready to join in devising such an amendment of the plan as will be most likely to secure our liberty and happiness."

July 9th. — " MR. DANIEL CARROLL [from Maryland] took his seat."

" MR. GOUVERNEUR MORRIS delivered a Report from the Committee of five members " [appointed on the 6th].

" MR. SHERMAN moved to refer the first part, apportioning Representatives, to a Committee of a member from each State."

---

* The "*value of land*" adopted in the Confederation as the rule to govern the States, in levying their respective proportions to supply the "common Treasury."

"Mr Gouverneur Morris seconded the motion. . . The Report is little more than a guess. Wealth was not altogether disregarded by the Committee. . . The Committee meant little more than to bring the matter to a point for the consideration of the House."

"Mr. Randolph disliked the Report of the Committee, but had been unwilling to object to it. . . He was in favor of a commitment to a member from each State."

"Mr. Butler urged warmly the justice and necessity of regarding wealth in the apportionment of Representatives."

On the question for committing to a member from each State, as moved by Mr. Sherman, *Aye*, nine ; *No*, two.

"The Committee appointed were Messrs. King, Sherman, Yates, Brearly, Gouverneur Morris, Read, Carroll, Madison, Williamson, Rutledge, Houston."

July 10*th*. — "Mr. King reported, from the Committee yesterday appointed, that the States, at the first meeting of the General Legislature, should be represented by sixty-five members ; . . to wit, — New Hampshire, by three ; Massachusetts, eight ; Rhode Island, one ; Connecticut, five ; New York, six ; New Jersey, four ; Pennsylvania, eight ; Delaware, one ; Maryland, six ; Virginia, ten ; North Carolina, five ; South Carolina, five ; Georgia, three."

"Mr. John Rutledge [from South Carolina] moved that New Hampshire be reduced from three to two members."

"General Pinckney seconds the motion."

"Mr. King. — New Hampshire has probably more than one hundred and twenty thousand inhabitants, and has an extensive country of tolerable fertility. Its inhabitants may therefore be expected to increase fast."

"General Pinckney. — The Report, before it was committed, was more favorable to the Southern States than as it now stands."

"Mr. Williamson was not for reducing New Hampshire from three to two, but for reducing some others."

"General Pinckney urged the reduction ; dwelt on the superior wealth of the Southern States, and insisted on its having its due weight in the Government."

"Mr. Gouverneur Morris regretted the *turn* of the debate. The States, he found, had many Representatives on the floor. Few, he feared, were to be deemed the Representatives of America. He thought the Southern States have by the Report, more than their share of representation. Property ought to have its weight, but not all the weight. . . He was against reducing New Hampshire."

On the question for reducing New Hampshire, from three to two Representatives, *Aye*, two ; *No*, eight.

It would seem hardly consistent to omit the insertion of the following significant letter, so illustrative of its author's views as to the proceedings and prospective issue of the Convention, — especially as to those parts of the proceedings which were the objects of the particular allusions it contains : —

GENERAL WASHINGTON *to* COLONEL HAMILTON.

"PHILADELPHIA, 10*th July*, 1787. ·

"DEAR SIR,—I thank you for your communication of the 3d instant. When I refer you to the state of the counsels which prevailed at the period you left this city [June 29th], and add that they are now, if possible, in a worse train than ever, you will find but little ground on which the hope of a good establishment can be formed. In a word, I almost despair of seeing a favorable issue to the proceedings of our Convention, and do therefore repent having had any agency in the business. The men who oppose a strong and energetic Government, are, in my opinion, narrow-minded politicians, or are under the influence of local views. The apprehension expressed by them, that the people will not accede to the form proposed, is *the ostensible, not the real*, cause of opposition. But, admitting that the present sentiment is as they prognosticate, the proper question ought nevertheless to be,—Is it, or is it not, the best form that such a country as this can adopt? If it be the best, recommend it; and it will assuredly obtain, maugre opposition. I am sorry you went away. I wish you were back. The crisis is equally important and alarming. No opposition, under such circumstances, should discourage exertions till the signature is offered. I will not at this time trouble you with more than my best wishes and sincere regard.

"I am, dear sir, etc." *

"GENERAL PINCKNEY, and MR. ALEXANDER MARTIN [from North Carolina], moved 'that six Representatives, instead of five,' be allowed to North Carolina."

On the question, *Aye*, three; *No*, seven.

"GENERAL PINCKNEY, and MR. PIERCE BUTLER [from South Carolina], made the same motion in favor of South Carolina."

On the question, *Aye*, four; *No*, seven.

"GENERAL PINCKNEY, and MR. WILLIAM HOUSTON [from Georgia], moved 'that Georgia be allowed four instead of three Representatives;' urging the unexampled celerity of its population."

On the question, *Aye*, four; *No*, seven.

On the question for agreeing to the appointment of Representatives, as amended by the last Committee, *Aye*, nine; *No*, two.

July 13*th*.—"MR. GOUVERNEUR MORRIS.—The train of business, and the late turn which it had taken, had led him into deep meditation on it; and he would candidly state the result. A distinction had been set up, and urged, between the Northern and Southern States. He had hitherto considered this doctrine as heretical. He still thought the distinction groundless. He sees, however, that it is persisted in; and the Southern gentlemen will not be satisfied, unless they see the way open to their gaining a majority in the public councils. The consequence of such a transfer of power from the maritime to the interior and landed interest, will, he foresees, be such an oppression to commerce, that he shall be

* It is recommended to re-examine, in connection with this letter, the extract of the one dated March 31st, 1783; p. 13. In this may be noticed a reference to one letter; and in that extract a reference to two, previously received from Colonel Hamilton. In them appears the same devoted and interested attention to the common cause, the same coincidence of political views, and the same concurrence of exertions to promote that cause, which characterzied all their correspondence from the spring of 1777.

The above letter may be found, in the "Writings of Washington," by Doctor Sparks, vol. ix. p. 260.

obliged to vote for the vicious principle of equality in the second branch, in order to provide some defence for the Northern States against it. . . . There can be no end of demands for security, if every particular interest is to be entitled to it. The Eastern States may claim it for . . . other objects, as the Southern States claim it for their peculiar objects. In this struggle between the two ends of the Union, what part ought the Middle States, in point of policy, to take? To join their Eastern brethren, according to his ideas."

July 14th. — " Mr. L. Martin called for the question on the whole Report, including the parts relating to the origination of money bills, and the equality of votes in the second branch."

" Mr. Rutledge proposed to reconsider the two propositions touching the originating of money bills in the first, and the equality of votes in the second branch."

" Mr. Sherman was for the question on the whole at once."

" Mr. L. Martin urged the question on the whole."

" Mr. Dayton. — The smaller States can never give up their equality. For himself, he would in no event yield that security for their rights."

" Mr. Sherman urged the equality of votes."

" Mr. King. — He considered the proposed Government as substantially and formally a General and National Government over the people of America. There never will be a case in which it will act as a Federal Government on the States and not on the individual citizens. And is it not a clear principle that, in a free government, those who are to be the objects of a government ought to influence the operations of it? . . . The General Government can never wish to intrude on the State Governments There could be no temptation. None had been pointed out. In order to prevent the interference of measures which seemed most likely to happen, he would have no objection to throwing all the State debts into the Federal debt, making one aggregate debt of about seventy million dollars, and leaving it to be discharged by the General Government. . . He was sure that no government would last that was not founded on just principles. He preferred the doing of nothing, to an allowance of an equal vote to all the States. It would be better, he thought, to submit to a little more confusion and convulsion, than to submit to such an evil."

" Mr. Strong. — The Convention had been much divided in opinion. In order to avoid the consequences of it, an accommodation had been proposed. A committee had been appointed. . . It is agreed, on all hands, that Congress are nearly at an end. If no accommodation takes place, the Union itself must soon be dissolved. . . He thought the small States had made a considerable concession, in the article of money bills, and that they might naturally expect some concessions on the other side. From this view of the matter, he was compelled to give his vote for the Report taken together."

" Mr. Madison expressed his apprehensions, that, if the proper foundation of government was destroyed, by substituting an equality in place of a proportional representation, no proper structure would be raised. . . He reminded them [the small States] of the consequences of laying the *existing Confederation* on improper principles. All the principal parties to its compilation joined immediately in mutilating and fettering the Government in such a manner, that it has disappointed every hope placed on it. He appealed to the doctrine and arguments used by themselves on a former occasion. . . He called for a single instance, in which the General Government was not to operate on the people individually. The practicability of making laws, with coercive sanctions. for the States as political bodies, had been exploded on all hands. . . No one would say that, in Congress or out of Congress, Delaware had equal weight with

Pennsylvania. . . It seemed now to be pretty well understood, that the real difference of interests lay, not between the large and small, but between the Northern and Southern States. The institution of slavery, and its consequences, formed the line of discrimination."

" MR. WILSON. — . . A vice in the representation, like an error in the first concoction, must be followed by disease, convulsions, and finally, death itself. The justice of the general principle of proportional representation has not, in argument at least, been yet contradicted. . . . The great fault of the existing Confederacy is its inactivity. . . To remedy this defect, we were sent here. Shall we effect the cure by establishing an equality of votes, as is proposed? No; this very equality carries us directly to Congress, — to the system which it is our duty to rectify."

July 16*th.* — " On the question for agreeing to the whole Report, as amended, and including the equality of votes in the second branch," *Aye,* five ; *No,* four.

" MR. RANDOLPH. — The vote of this morning (involving an equality of suffrage in the second branch) had embarrassed the business extremely. All the powers given in the Report from the Committee of the Whole were founded on the supposition that a proportional representation was to prevail in both branches of the Legislature. . . . He could not but think we were unprepared to discuss this subject further. . . He wished the Convention to adjourn, that the large States might consider the steps proper to be taken, in the present solemn crisis of the business ; and that the small States might also deliberate on the means of conciliation."

" MR. PATTERSON. — No conciliation could be admissible, on the part of the smaller States, on any other ground than that of an equality of votes in the second branch. If MR. RANDOLPH would reduce to form his motion for an adjournment *sine die,* he would second it with all his heart."

" MR. RANDOLPH had never entertained an idea of an adjournment *sine die ;* and was sorry that his meaning had been so readily and strangely misinterpreted. He had in view merely an adjournment till tomorrow, in order that some conciliatory experiment might, if possible, be devised.''

" MR. PATTERSON seconded the adjournment till tomorrow ; as an opportunity seemed to be wished by the larger States to deliberate further on conciliatory expedients."

" MR. BROOM thought it his duty to declare his opinion against an adjournment *sine die,* as had been urged by MR. PATTERSON. Such a measure, he thought, would be fatal. Something must be done by the Convention, though it should be by a bare majority."

" MR. RUTLEDGE could see no need of an adjournment, because he could see no chance of a compromise. The little States were fixed. They had repeatedly and solemnly declared themselves to be so. All the large States, then, had to do, was to decide whether they would yield or not. For his part, he conceived, that, although we could not do what we thought best in itself, we ought to do something."

" MR. RANDOLPH and MR. KING renewed the motion to adjourn till tomorrow."

On the question, *Aye,* seven ; *No,* two.
The Convention accordingly adjourned.
From MR. MADISON's description, as follows, the result of the adjournment appears to have greatly disappointed the mover and several others : —

" On the morning following, before the hour of the Convention, a number of the members . . met for the purpose of consulting on the proper steps to be taken. . . The time was wasted in vague conversation on the subject . . It appeared, indeed, that the opinions of the members, who disliked the equality of votes, differed much as to the importance of that point, and as to the policy of risking a failure of any general act of the Convention by inflexibly opposing it. Several of them, supposing that no good government could or would be built on that foundation, ... would have concurred in a firm opposition to the smaller States, and on a separate recommendation, if eventually necessary. Others seemed inclined to yield to the smaller States, and to concur in such an act, however imperfect and exceptionable, as might be agreed on by the Convention as a body, though decided by a bare majority of States and by a minority of the people of the United States." *

July 17*th.* — " MR. GOUVERNEUR MORRIS moved to reconsider the whole Resolution agreed to yesterday concerning the constitution of the two branches of the Legislature."

MR. MADISON states that " This motion was not seconded; but was probably approved by several members, who either despaired of success, or were apprehensive that the attempt would inflame the jealousies of the smaller States."

The clause, — " To negative all laws passed by the several States contravening, in the opinion of the National Legislature, the Articles of Union, or any treaties subsisting under the authority of the Union," — was taken up.

" MR. MADISON considered the negative on the laws of the States as essential to the efficacy and security of the General Government. The necessity of a General Government proceeds from the propensity of the States to pursue their particular interests, in opposition to the general interest. This propensity will continue to disturb the system unless effectually controlled. Nothing short of a negative on their laws will control it. . . Confidence cannot be put in the State tribunals as guardians of the National authority and interests."

" MR. PINCKNEY urged the necessity of the negative." †

" On the question for agreeing to the power, *Aye*, three; *No*, seven."

The clause — " That a National Executive be instituted, to consist of a single person," — was agreed to, *nem. con.*

The next clause, — " To be chosen by the National Legislature," — being considered, —

" MR. GOUVERNEUR MORRIS was pointedly against his being so chosen. He will be the mere creature of the Legislature. . . . He ought to be elected by the people at large. . . He moved to strike out ' National Legislature,' and insert 'citizens of the United States.' "

" MR. SHERMAN thought that the sense of the Nation would be better expressed by the Legislature, than by the people at large."

" COLONEL MASON. — . . . . He conceived it would be as unnatural to refer the choice of a proper character for Chief Magistrate to the people, as it would, to refer a trial of colors to a blind man."

* This crisis, on the 16th of July, is worthy of particular notice, as having probably appeared then even more solemn and appalling than that, on the 2nd; as seen, p. 32.
† See Mr. Pinckney's motion, seconded by Mr. Madison, *June* 8*th;* p. 16.

On the question for an election by the people, instead of the Legislature, *Aye*, one ; *No*, nine.

On the question, "to be chosen by the National Legislature," *Aye*, unanimously.

On the question, "For the term of seven years, to be ineligible a second time,"—

"MR. HOUSTON moved to strike out, 'to be ineligible a second time.'"

On the question for striking out, as moved by MR. HOUSTON, *Aye*, six ; *No*, four.

The clause, "for the term of seven years," being resumed,—

"DOCTOR JAMES McCLURG [of Virginia], moved to strike out 'seven years,' and insert 'during good behavior.' By striking out the words, declaring him ineligible [a second time], he was put into a situation that would keep him dependent forever on the Legislature ; and he conceived the independence of the Executive to be equally essential with that of the Judiciary department."

"MR. GOUVERNEUR MORRIS seconded the motion. He expressed great pleasure in hearing it. This was the way to get a good Government."

"MR. BROOM highly approved the motion. It obviated all his difficulties."

"MR. MADISON.—If it be essential to the preservation of liberty, that the Legislative, Executive, and Judiciary powers be separate, it is essential to a maintenance of the separation, that they should be independent of each other. The Executive could not be independent of the Legislature, if dependent on the pleasure of that branch for a reappointment. . . There was an analogy between the Executive and Judiciary departments in several respects. . . It might be more dangerous to suffer a union between the Executive and Legislative powers, than between the Judiciary and Legislative powers. He conceived it to be absolutely necessary to a well constituted Republic, that the two first should be kept distinct and independent of each other."

"COLONEL MASON.—He considered an Executive during good behavior as a softer name only, for an Executive for life ; and that the next would be an easy step to hereditary monarchy. If the motion should finally succeed, he might himself live to see such a revolution. . . No State, he was sure, had so far revolted from Republican principles, as to have the least bias in its favor."

"MR. MADISON was not apprehensive of being thought to favor any step towards monarchy. The real object with him, was to prevent its introduction."

"MR. GOUVERNEUR MORRIS was as little a friend to monarchy as any gentleman. He concurred in the opinion, that the way to keep out monarchical government, was to establish such a Republican government as would make the people happy, and prevent a desire of change."

"DOCTOR McCLURG was not so much afraid of the shadow of monarchy, as to be unwilling to approach it ; nor so wedded to Republican government, as not to be sensible of the tyrannies that had been, and may be, exercised under that form." *

July 18*th.*—The Resolution,—"That the National Legislature be empowered to appoint inferior tribunals,"—being taken up,—

From the writings of General Washington, Mr. Madison, and Mr. Jefferson, Doctor McClurg appears to have been considered as possessing talents and attainments of the highest order.

"Mr. Butler could see no necessity for such tribunals. The State tribunals might do the business."

"Mr. L. Martin concurred. They will create jealousies and oppositions in the State tribunals, with the jurisdiction of which they will interfere."

"Mr. Gorham. — There are in the States already Federal Courts, with jurisdiction for trial of piracies, etc. No complaints have been made by the States, or the Courts of the States Inferior tribunals are essential to render the authority of the National Legislature effectual."

"Mr. Randolph observed, that the Courts of the States cannot be trusted with the administration of the National laws."

"Mr. Gouverneur Morris urged also the necessity of such a provision."

"Mr. Sherman was willing to give the power to the Legislature, but wished them to make use of the State tribunals, whenever it could be done with safety to the general interest."

On the question " for empowering the National Legislature to appoint inferior tribunals," agreed to, *nem. con.*

"Mr. Madison moved ' that the constitutional authority of the States ' shall be guaranteed to them, respectively, against domestic as well as foreign violence."

"Doctor McClurg seconded the motion."

"Mr. Houston was afraid of perpetuating the existing Constitutions of the States. That of Georgia is a very bad one, and [he] hoped [it] would be revised and amended. It may also be difficult for the General Government to decide between contending parties, each of which claim the sanction of the Constitution."

"Mr. L. Martin was for leaving the States to suppress rebellions themselves."

"Mr. Gorham thought it strange, that a rebellion should be known to exist in the Empire, and the General Government should be restrained from interposing to subdue it. . . . With regard to different parties in a State, as long as they confine their disputes to words, they will be harmless to the General Government, and to each other. If they appeal to the sword, it will then be necessary for the General Government, however difficult it may be to decide on the merits of their contest, to interpose, and put an end to it."

"Mr. Carroll. — Some such provision is essential. Every State ought to wish for it."

"Mr. Wilson moved, as a better expression of the idea, that a republican form of Government shall be guaranteed to each State; and that each State shall be protected against foreign and domestic violence."

On the question, — " for agreeing to Mr. Wilson's motion," — it passed, *nem. con.*

July 19th. — "Mr. L. Martin moved [in regard to the tenure of the Executive office] to reinstate the words, — ' to be ineligible a second time.' "

"Mr. Gouverneur Morris. — It is necessary to take into one view all that relates to the establishment of the Executive. . . Our country is an extensive one. We must either, then, renounce the blessings of the Union, or provide an Executive with sufficient vigor to pervade every part of it. . . . . The Executive, therefore, ought to be so constituted as to be the great protector of the mass of the people. It is the duty of the Executive to appoint the officers, and to command the forces, of the Republic; to appoint, first, ministerial officers for the administration of public affairs; secondly, officers for the dispensation of justice. Who will be the best judges whether these appointments be well made? The people at large; who will know, will see, will feel, the effects of them. Again, who can judge so well of the discharge of military duties, for the protection and security of the people, as the people themselves, who are to be protected and secured? . . . If he is to be the guardian of the people, let him be appointed by the people. . . It has been said, that the candidates for this office will not be known to the people. If they be known to the Legislature, they must have such a notoriety and eminence of character, that they cannot possibly be unknown to the people at large. . . It deserved consideration, also, that such an ingredient in the plan would render it extremely palatable to the people. These were the general ideas which occurred to him on the subject, and led him to wish and move, that the whole constitution of the Executive might undergo reconsideration."

" MR. WILSON. — . . He perceived, with pleasure, that the idea was gaining ground of an election, mediately or immediately, by the people " [rather than by the Legislature].

"MR. MADISON. — . . There is the same, perhaps greater, reason why the Executive should be independent of the Legislature, than why the Judiciary should. A coalition of the two former powers would be more immediately and certainly dangerous to public liberty. It is essential, then, that the appointment of the Executive should either be drawn from some source, or held by some tenure, that will give him a free agency with regard to the Legislature. This could not be, if he was to be appointable, from time to time, by the Legislature. . . . . He was disposed, for these reasons, to refer the appointment to some other source. The people at large was, in his opinion, the fittest in itself. . . . There was one difficulty, however, of a serious nature, attending an immediate choice by the people. The right of suffrage was much more diffusive in the Northern than in the Southern States; and the latter could have no influence in the election on the score of the negroes. The substitution of Electors obviated this difficulty, and seemed, on the whole, liable to the fewest objections."

" MR. GERRY. — . . He was against a popular election. The people are uninformed, and would be misled by a few designing men. . . The popular mode of electing the Chief Magistrate would certainly be the worst of all."

On the question, on MR. GOUVERNEUR MORRIS's motion, — " To reconsider generally the constitution of the Executive," — *Aye*, unanimously.

July 23d. — " MR. JOHN LANGDON and MR. NICHOLAS GILMAN, from New Hampshire, took their seats."

The Resolution, — " Referring the new Constitution to Assemblies, to be chosen by the people, for the express purpose of ratifying it," — was taken into consideration.

" MR. ELLSWORTH moved, that it be referred to the Legislatures of the States for ratification."

" MR. PATTERSON seconded the motion."

" COLONEL MASON considered a reference of the plan to the authority of the people as one of the most important and essential of the Resolutions. The Legislatures have no power to ratify it. They are the mere creatures of the State Constitutions, and cannot be greater than their creators."

"Mr. Randolph.—One idea has pervaded all our proceedings; to wit, that opposition, as well from the States as from individuals, will be made to the system proposed. . . Whose opposition will be most likely to be excited against the system? That of the local demagogues, who will be degraded by it from the importance they now hold. These will spare no efforts to impede that progress in the popular mind which will be necessary to the adoption of the plan, and which every member will find to have taken place in his own, if he will compare his present opinions with those he brought with him into the Convention. It is of great importance, therefore, that the consideration of this subject should be transferred from the Legislatures, where this class of men have their full influence, to a field in which their efforts can be less mischievous."

"Mr. Gerry.— . . Great confusion, he was confident, would result from a recurrence to the people. They would never agree on anything. He could not see any ground to suppose that the people will do what their rulers will not. The rulers will either conform to, or influence the sense of, the people."

"Mr. Gorham was against referring the plan to the Legislatures. Men chosen by the people for the particular purpose will discuss the subject more candidly than members of the Legislature, who are to lose the power which is to be given up to the General Government. . . In the States, many of the ablest men are excluded from the Legislatures, but may be elected into a Convention. Among these may be ranked many of the clergy, who are generally friends to good government. Their services were found to be valuable in the formation and establishment of the Constitution of Massachusetts. . . If the last Article of the Confederation is to be pursued, the unanimous concurrence of the States will be necessary. It would, therefore, deserve serious consideration, whether provision ought not to be made for giving effect to the system without waiting for the unanimous concurrence of the States."

"Mr. Gouverneur Morris.—If the Confederation is to be pursued, no alteration can be made without the unanimous consent of the Legislatures. . . . Whereas, in case of an appeal to the people of the United States, the supreme authority, the Federal compact may be altered by a *majority of them*, in like manner as the Constitution of a particular State may be altered by a majority of the people of the State. The amendment moved by Mr. Ellsworth erroneously supposes that we are proceeding on the basis of the Confederation. This Convention is unknown to the Confederation."

"Mr. King.—He preferred a reference to the authority of the people, expressly delegated to Conventions, as the most certain means of obviating all disputes and doubts concerning the legitimacy of the new Constitution, as well as the most likely means of drawing forth the best men in the States to decide on it. . . . He considered it as of some consequence, also, to get rid of the scruples which some members of the State Legislatures might derive from their oaths to support and maintain the existing Constitutions."

"Mr. Madison thought it clear that the Legislatures were incompetent to the proposed changes. These changes would make essential inroads on the State Constitutions. . . He considered the difference between a system founded on the [State] Legislatures only, and one founded on the people, to be the true difference between a *league* or *treaty*, and a *Constitution*. The former, in point of *moral obligation*, might be as inviolable as the latter. In point of *political operation*, there were two important distinctions in favor of the latter. . Comparing the two modes, in point of expediency, he thought all the considerations which recommended this Convention, in preference to Congress, for proposing the reform, were in favor of State Conventions, in preference to the Legislatures for examining and adopting it."

On the question, for MR. ELLSWORTH's motion [seconded by MR. PATTERSON], "to refer the plan to the Legislatures of the States," *Aye*, three; *No*, seven.

"MR. GOUVERNEUR MORRIS moved [as according with his ideas concerning the extent of the interests involved], that the reference of the plan be made to one general Convention, chosen and authorized by the people to consider, amend, and establish the same."

On the question for agreeing to the Resolution,— . . . "To refer the Constitution . . . to Assemblies chosen by the people,"—*Aye*, nine; *No*, one.

"MR. GERRY moved, that the proceedings of the Convention for the establishment of a National Government (except the parts relating to the Executive) be referred to a Committee to prepare and report a Constitution conformable thereto."

"GENERAL PINCKNEY reminded the Convention, that, if the Committee should fail to insert some security to the Southern States against the emancipation of slaves, and taxes on exports, he should be bound by duty to his State to vote against their Report."

"The appointment of a Committee, as moved by MR. GERRY, was agreed to," *nem. con.*

July 24th.—"On a ballot, . . . the members chosen were:—MR. RUTLEDGE, MR. RANDOLPH, MR. GORHAM, MR. ELLSWORTH, MR. WILSON."

July 25th.—The clause "relating to the Executive" being again under consideration,—

"MR. WILLIAMSON.—The principal objection against an election by the people seemed to be, the disadvantage under which it would place the smaller States. He suggested, as a cure for this difficulty, that each man should vote for three candidates; one of them, he observed, would be probably of his own State, the other two of some other States; and as probably of a small as a large one."

"MR. GOUVERNEUR MORRIS liked the idea; MR. MADISON also thought something valuable might be made of the suggestion."

"MR. GERRY.—A popular election in this case is radically vicious. The ignorance of the people would put it in the power of some one set of men dispersed through the Union, and acting in concert, to delude them into any appointment. He observed that such a society of men existed in the Order of the Cincinnati. . . They will, in fact, elect the Chief Magistrate in every instance, if the election be referred to the people. His respect for the characters composing this Society could not blind him to the danger and impropriety of throwing such a power into their hands."

"MR. JOHN DICKINSON.—He had long leaned towards an election by the people, which he regarded as the best and purest source. Objections, he was aware, lay against this mode, but not so great, he thought, as against the other modes. The greatest difficulty, in the opinion of the House, seemed to arise from the partiality of the States to their respective citizens."

July 26th.—"COLONEL MASON.—In every stage of the question relative to the Executive, the difficulty of the subject, and the diversity of opinions

concerning it, have appeared. . . . A popular election, in any form, as MR. GERRY has observed, would throw the appointment into the hands of the Cincinnati; a society, for the members of which he had a great respect, but which he never wished to have a proponderating influence in the Government. . . . .
He concluded with moving that the constitution of the Executive, as reported by the Committee of the Whole, be reinstated; namely, 'that the Executive be appointed for seven years, and be ineligble a second time.' "

" MR. DAVIE seconded the motion."

On the question, *Aye*, seven; *No*, three.

" MR. GOUVERNEUR MORRIS was now against the whole paragraph."

On the question for the whole Resolution, as amended, — " That a National Executive be instituted, to consist of a single person, to be chosen by the National Legislature, for the term of seven years, to be ineligble a second time," — " New Hampshire, Connecticut, New Jersey, North Carolina, South Carolina, Georgia, *Aye*, six; Pennsylvania, Delaware, Maryland, *No*, three; Massachusetts, not on the floor; Virginia, divided, — MR. BLAIR and COLONEL MASON, *Aye;* GENERAL WASHINGTON and MR. MADISON, *No*. MR. RANDOLPH happened to be out of the house."

" COLONEL MASON moved, that the Committee of Detail be instructed to receive a clause requiring certain qualifications of landed property, and citizenship of the United States, in members of the National Legislature, and disqualifying persons having unsettled accounts with, or being indebted to, the United States, from being members of the National Legislature."

" MR. GOUVERNEUR MORRIS. — If qualifications are proper, he would prefer them in the electors, rather than the elected. As to debtors of the United States, they are few. As to persons having unsettled accounts, he believed them to be pretty many. He thought, however, such a discrimination to be both odious and useless, and, in many instances, unjust and cruel. The delay of settlement had been more the fault of the public, than of the individuals. What will be done with those patriotic citizens who have lent money, or services, or property, to their country, without having been yet able to obtain a liquidation of their claims? Are they to be excluded? "

" MR. GORHAM was for leaving to the Legislature the providing against such abuses as had been mentioned."

" MR. MADISON. — . . It might be well to limit the exclusion to persons who had received money from the public, and had not accounted for it."

" MR. GERRY thought the inconvenience of excluding a few worthy individuals, . . ought not to be put in the scale against the public advantages of the regulation, and that the motion did not go far enough."

" MR. DICKINSON. — It seemed improper that any man of merit should be subjected to disabilities in a republic, where merit was understood to form the great title to public trust, honors, and rewards."

" MR. GERRY. — If property be one object of government, provisions to secure it cannot be improper."

" MR. WILSON. — We should consider that we are providing a Constitution for future generations, and not merely for the peculiar circumstances of the moment. The time has been, and will again be, when the public safety may depend on the voluntary aids of individuals, which will necessarily open accounts with the public; and when such accounts will be a characteristic of patriotism. Besides, a partial enumeration of cases will disable the Legislature from disqualifying odious and dangerous characters.''

" MR. LANGDON was for striking out the whole clause, for the reasons given by MR. WILSON. So many exclusions, he thought, too, would render the system unacceptable to the people.''

" MR. GERRY. — If the arguments used today were to prevail, we might have a Legislature composed of public debtors, pensioners, placemen, and contractors. He thought the proposed disqualifications would be pleasing to the people. . . He moved to add ' pensioners ' to the disqualified characters.''

On the question, *Aye*, three; *No*, seven.

" MR. GOUVERNEUR MORRIS. — He repeated, that it had not been so much the fault of individuals, as of the public, that transactions between them had not been more generally liquidated and adjusted. At all events, to draw from our short and scanty experience, rules that are to operate through succeeding ages, does not savor much of real wisdom.''

On the question for striking out, as moved by MR. LANGDON, *Aye*, nine; *No*, two.

On the question for agreeing to the clause " disqualifying public debtors," *Aye*, two; *No*, nine.

It has been shown (p. 45), that, on the 23d, the Convention voted unanimously to appoint a Committee, " to prepare and report a Constitution, conformable to " the Resolutions which they had adopted; that, on the 24th, they appointed that Committee, consisting of five members; and that they then voted to discharge the Committee of the Whole from the propositions submitted by MR. C. PINCKNEY, on the 29th of May, and refer them, and also those offered by MR. PATTERSON, on the 15th of June, " to the Committee of Detail just appointed." On the 26th, they voted to refer likewise their proceedings since the 23rd to the same Committee.

The Convention adjourned, soon after, " till August 6th, that the Committee might have time to prepare and report the Constitution."

Such is a summary view of the manner in which the Convention were occupied six weeks in considering and acting upon the Resolutions of MR. RANDOLPH, as those Resolutions had, in two weeks, been amended and agreed to in Committee of the Whole, and reported to the House on the 13th of June (as seen, p. 18).

Considering the striking contrast of views and opinions which were so repeatedly and threateningly exhibited; considering also that the question of slavery was yet to be taken up, for the first time, as a special matter to be disposed of; and considering, moreover, that a review of the subjects already under debate, together with the consideration of others afterward introduced, protracted the debates through an additional period of more than seven weeks, — it seems wonderful, that they were enabled to reach any practical issue whatever; and still more wonderful, that they finally reached an issue, so productive of unparalleled blessings, not only to themselves and their generation, but to successive generations after them.

———————

At this stage of the work, it is deemed appropriate to append to what has been presented in the preceding pages, the following testimony of MR. MADISON : —

" Whatever may be the judgment pronounced on the architects of the Constitution, or whatever may be the destiny of the edifice prepared by them, I feel it a duty to express my profound and solemn conviction, derived from my intimate opportunity of observing and appreciating the views of the Convention, collectively and individually, that there never was an assembly of men, charged with a great and arduous trust, who were more pure in their motives, or more exclusively, or more anxiously devoted to the object committed to them, than were the members of the Federal Convention of 1787, to the object of devising and proposing a constitutional system, which should best supply the defects of that which it was to replace, and best secure the permanent liberty and happiness of their country."

August 6th. — MR. JOHN FRANCIS MERCER took his seat in that body, as stated in the note to the preceding p. 3.

According to appointment when the Convention adjourned, the Committee of Detail, by their chairman, MR. RUTLEDGE, delivered in their Report; a copy of which was furnished to each member.

" A motion was made to adjourn, in order to give leisure to examine the Report."

" The House then adjourned till tomorrow at eleven o'clock."

In compliance with their instructions, their Report was the draft of a Constitution, and from that time during the session of the Convention, their debates related to the provisions it contained, or to such others as were proposed. Those instructions, and the several documents referred to them for their guidance in forming it, were designated in p. 47.

Of the proceedings in the Convention from this date to the 14th, the portions deemed specially adapted to the original and present design of this work, were given in the preceding pp. 1 — 4; to which the reader is referred.

August 14th. — Section 1st of Article VI., in the Report, viz. : — " The members of each House shall receive a compensation for their services, to be ascertained and paid by the State in which they shall be chosen," being taken up, —

" MR. ELLSWORTH said that, in reflecting on the subject, he had been satisfied that too much dependence would be produced by that mode of payment. He moved to strike out and insert, that they should be paid out of the Treasury of the United States, an allowance not exceeding —— dollars per day." *

" MR. GOUVERNEUR MORRIS moved that the payment be out of the National Treasury; leaving the quantum to the National Legislature. There could be no reason to fear that they would overpay themselves."

" MR. BUTLER contended for payment by the States; particularly in the case of the Senate."

" MR. LANGDON was against payment by the States."

" MR. MADISON. — If the House of Representatives is to be chosen *biennially*, and the Senate to be constantly dependent on the Legislatures [of the States], which are chosen *annually*, he could not see any chance for that stability in the General Government, the want of which was a principal evil in the State Governments. His fear was, that the organization of the Government, supposing the Senate to be really independent for six years, would not effect our purpose."

" MR. BROOM could see no danger in trusting the General Legislature with the payment of themselves. The State Legislatures had this power, and no complaint had been made of it."

" MR. SHERMAN . . thought the best plan would be, to fix a moderate allowance to be paid out of the National Treasury, and let the States make such additions as they might judge fit."

* See Mr. Ellsworth's former expressions on the subject, pp. 24, 27.

"Mr. Carroll had been much surprised at seeing this clause in the Report. The dependence of both Houses on the State Legislatures is complete. . . . The new Government in this form was nothing more than a second edition of Congress, in two volumes instead of one, and, perhaps, with very few amendments."

"Mr. Dickinson took it for granted that all were convinced of the necessity of making the General Government independent of the prejudices, passions, and improper views, of the State Legislatures. The contrary of this was effected by the section as it stands. . . . . If the General Gov rnment should be left dependent on the State Legislatures, it would be happy for us if we had never met in this room."

"Mr. Ellsworth was not unwilling himself to trust the Legislature with authority to regulate their own wages ; but well knew that an unlimited discretion for that purpose would produce strong. though perhaps not insuperable, objections [to the contemplated Government]."

"Mr. L. Martin.—As the Senate is to represent the States, the members of it ought to be paid by the States."

"Mr. Carroll. — The Senate was to represent and manage the affairs of the whole, and not to be the advocates of State interests. They ought, then, not to be dependent on, nor paid by, the States."

"On the question for paying the members of the Legislature out of the National Treasury, — *Aye*, nine ; *No*, two."

"It was moved and agreed to amend the section by adding, '. to be ascertained by law.'"

"The section, as amended, was then agreed to, *nem. con.*"

August 17*th.* — The clause, "to subdue a rebellion in any State on the application of its Legislature," was considered.

"Mr. Pinckney moved to strike out, ' on the application of its Legislature.' "

"Mr. Gouverneur Morris seconds."

"Mr. L. Martin opposed it, as giving a dangerous and unnecessary power. The consent of the State ought to precede the introduction of any extraneous force whatever."

"Mr. Ellsworth proposed to add after Legislature, 'or Executive.' "

"Mr. Gouverneur Morris. — The General Government should enforce obedience in all cases where it may be necessary."

"Mr. Ellsworth. — . . . He was willing to vary his motion so as to read, ' or without it,' when the Legislature cannot meet."

"Mr. Gerry was against letting loose the myrmidons of the United States without its consent. The States will be the best judges in such cases."

"Mr. Langdon was for striking out, as moved by Mr. Pinckney. The apprehension of the National force will have a salutary effect, in preventing insurrections."

"Mr. Randolph. — If the National Legislature is to judge whether the State Legislatures can or cannot meet, that amendment would make the clause as objectionable as the motion of Mr. Pinckney."

"Mr. Gouverneur Morris. — We are acting a very strange part. We first form a strong man to protect us, and at the same time wish to tie his hands behind him. The Legislature may surely be trusted with such a power to preserve the public tranquillity.'"

"On the motion to add 'or without it [application] when the Legislature cannot meet,'—*Aye*, five ; *No*, three."

August 18*th.* — " MR. RUTLEDGE moved to refer [to the Committee of Detail] a clause, 'that funds appropriated to public creditors should not be diverted to other purposes.'"

" MR. MASON was much attached to the principle, but was afraid such a fetter might be dangerous in time of war. He suggested the necessity of preventing the danger of perpetual revenue."

" MR. RUTLEDGE's motion was referred. He then moved that a Grand Committee be appointed to consider the necessity and expediency of the United States assuming all the State debts. . . . The assumption would be just; as the State debts were contracted in the common defence. . . . It would be politic ; as, by disburthening the people of the State debts, it would conciliate them to the plan."

" MR. KING and MR. PINCKNEY seconded the motion."

" MR. KING.— . . Besides the considerations of justice and policy which have been mentioned, it might be remarked that the State creditors, an active and formidable party, would otherwise be opposed to a plan which transferred to the Union the best resources, . . . without transferring the State debts at the same time. . . . He would not say that it was practicable to consolidate the debts, but he thought it would be prudent to have the subject considered by a Committee."

" MR. RUTLEDGE's motion, 'that a Committee be appointed to consider of the assumption,' etc., was agreed to.—*Aye*, six ; *No*, four."

" MR. KING suggested that all unlocated lands of particular States ought to be given up."

" MR. WILLIAMSON concurred in the idea."

"A Grand Committee [according to MR. RUTLEDGE's motion] was then appointed, consisting of MR. LANGDON, MR. KING, MR. SHERMAN, MR. LIVINGSTON, MR. CLYMER, MR. DICKINSON, MR. McHENRY, MR. MASON, MR. WILLIAMSON, MR. C. C. PINCKNEY, and MR. BALDWIN."

" The House proceeded to the clause, 'to raise armies.'"

" MR. GORHAM moved to add 'and support,' after 'raise.' Agreed to, *nem. con.*"

" Then the clause, as amended, was agreed to, *nem. con.*"

" MR. GERRY took notice that there was no check here against standing armies in time of peace. . . . The people were jealous on this head, and great opposition to the plan would spring from such an omission. . He thought an army dangerous in time of peace, and could never consent to a power to keep up an indefinite number. He proposed that there should not be kept up in time of peace more than —— thousand troops. His idea was; that the blank should be filled with two or three thousand."

"A clause, 'to make rules for the government and regulation of the land and naval forces,' was added from the existing Articles of Confederation."

"Mr. L. Martin, and Mr. Gerry, now regularly moved, ' provided that in time of peace, the army shall not consist of more than ——— thousand men.' "

"General Pinckney asked, whether no troops were ever to be raised until an attack should be made on us?"

"Mr. Gerry. — If there be no restriction, a few States may establish a military Government."

"Mr. Langdon saw no room for Mr. Gerry's distrust of the Representatives of the people."

"Mr. Dayton. — Preparations for war are generally made in time of peace ; and a standing force of some sort may, for aught we know, become unavoidable. He should object to no restriction consistent with these ideas."

"The motion of Mr. Martin and Mr. Gerry was disagreed to, *nem. con.*"

"Mr. Mason moved, as an additional power, 'to make laws for the regulation and discipline of the militia of the several States, reserving to the States the appointment of the officers.' "

"Mr. Pinckney mentioned a case during the [Revolutionary] war, in which a dissimilarity in the militia of different States had produced the most serious mischiefs. Uniformity was essential. The States will never keep up a proper discipline of the militia."

"Mr. Mason had suggested the idea of a select militia. He was led to think that would be, in fact, as much as the General Government co ild advantageously be charged with. He was afraid of creating insuperable objections to the plan."

"General Pinckney renewed Mr. Mason's original motion.* For a part to be under the General Government, and a part under the State Governments, would be an incurable evil. He saw no room for such distrust of the General Government."

"Mr. Langdon seconds General Pinckney's renewal. He saw no more reason to be afraid of the General Government than of the State Governments. He was more apprehensive of the confusion of the different authorities on this subject, than of either."

"Mr. Madison thought the regulation of the militia naturally appertaining to the authority charged with the public defence. It did not seem, in its nature, to be divisible between two distinct authorities. . . Those who had a full view of the public situation, would, from a sense of the danger, guard against it. The States would not be separately impressed with the general situation, nor have the due confidence in the concurrent exertions of each other."

"Mr. Pinckney thought the power such an one as could not be abused, and that the States would see the necessity of surrendering it. He had, however. but a scanty faith in militia. There must be also a real military force. This alone can effectually answer the pu: pose. The United States

* Mr. Mason's original motion was, to refer to the Committee, "a power to regulate the militia."

has been making an experiment without it, and we see the consequence in their rapid approaches toward anarchy."   •

" Mr. Gerry thought this the last point remaining to be surrendered. If it be agreed to by the Convention, the plan will have as black a mark as was set on Cain. He had no such confidence in the General Government as some gentlemen possessed, and believed it would be found the States have not."

" Mr. Read doubted the propriety of leaving the appointment of the militia officers to the States."

" On the question for committing to the Grand Committee, last appointed, the latter motion of Colonel Mason, and the original one revived by General Pinckney, *Aye*, eight; *No*, two. Maryland, divided."

August 20th. — Mr. Pinckney submitted to the House, in order to be referred to the Committee of Detail, a number of propositions, two of which were the following:—

" The United States shall be forever considered as one body corporate and politic in law, and entitled to all the rights, privileges and immunities which to bodies corporate do or ought to appertain."

" The jurisdiction of the Supreme Court shall be extended to all controversies between the United States and an individual State; or, the United States and the citizens of an individual State."

" These propositions were referred to the Committee of Detail, without debate or consideration of them by the House."

" Colonel Mason moved to enable Congress 'to enact sumptuary laws.' No Government can be maintained, unless the manners be made consonant to it. Such a discretionary power may do good, and can do no harm."

On this motion, as to " sumptuary laws," *Aye*, three; *No*, eight.

" The clause, 'to make all laws necessary and proper for carrying into execution the foregoing powers, and all other powers vested by this Constitution in the Government of the United States, or any department or officer thereof,'— was agreed to, *nem. con.*"

" The Section concerning treason, was then taken up."

" Doctor Johnson. — . . He contended that treason could not be both against the United States, and individual States; being an offence against the sovereignty, which can be but one in the same community."

" Mr. Ellsworth. — There can be no danger to the general authority, as the laws of the United States are to be paramount."

" Doctor Johnson was still of opinion there could be no treason against a particular State. It could not, even at present, as the Confederation now stands, the sovereignty being in the Union; much less can it be under the proposed system."

" COLONEL MASON. — . . The individual States will retain a part of the sovereignty. An act may be treason against a particular State, which is not so against the United States. He cited the rebellion of Bacon, in Virginia, as an illustration of the doctrine."

" DOCTOR JOHNSON. — That case would amount to treason against the sovereign, the supreme sovereign, the United States."

" MR KING. — No line can be drawn between levying war and adhering to the enemy against the United States, and against an individual State. Treason against the latter must be so against the former."

" MR. SHERMAN. — Resistance against the laws of the United States, as distinguished from resistance against the laws of a particular State, forms the line."

" MR. ELLSWORTH. — The United States are sovereign on one side of the line — the States on the other."

" MR. DICKINSON. — War or insurrection against a member of the Union, must be so against the whole body."

After several amendments, the " section was agreed to, *nem. con.*"

August 21st. — The clause, — " No tax or duty shall be laid by the Legislature on articles exported from any State," — was taken up.

" MR. LANGDON. — By this section the States are left at liberty to tax exports. New Hampshire, therefore, with other non-exporting States, will be subject to be taxed by the States exporting its produce."

" MR. ELLSWORTH. — . . . The power of regulating trade between the States will protect them against each other."

" MR. WILLIAMSON. — . . . He would never agree to this power. Should it take place, it would destroy the last hope of the adoption of the plan."

" MR. GOUVERNEUR MORRIS. — These local considerations ought not to impede the general interest. There is great weight in the argument, that the exporting States will tax the produce of their uncommercial neighbors. The power of regulating the trade between Pennsylvania and New Jersey, will never prevent the former from taxing the latter. [But] if no tax can be laid on exports, an embargo cannot be laid; though, in time of war, such a measure may be of critical importance. Tobacco, lumber, and live-stock, are three objects belonging to different States, of which great advantage might be made by a [general] power to tax exports. To these may be added ginseng, and masts for ships, by which a tax might be thrown on other nations. . . The state of the country, also, will change, and render duties on exports, as skins, beaver, and other peculiar raw materials, politic in the view of encouraging American manufactures."

" MR. BUTLER was strenuously opposed to a power over exports, as unjust, and alarming to the Staple States [meaning the Southern States]."

" MR. DICKINSON. — The power of taxing exports may be inconvenient at present; but it must be of dangerous consequence to prohibit it, with respect to all articles and forever."

" MR. SHERMAN. — It is best to prohibit the National Legislature in all cases. The States will never give up all power over trade."

" MR. MADISON. — As we ought to be governed by National and permanent views, it is a sufficient argument for giving the power over exports, that a tax, though it may not be expedient at present, may be so hereafter. A proper regulation of exports may, and probably will, be necessary hereafter, and for the same purposes as the regulation of imports ; viz., for revenue, domestic manufactures, and procuring equitable regulations from other nations.''

" Mr. WILSON. — Pennsylvania exports the produce of Maryland, New Jersey, Delaware, and will, by and by, when the River Delaware is opened, export for New York. In favoring the general power over exports, therefore, he opposed the particular interest of his State. . . To deny this power, is to take from the common Government half the regulation of trade. It was his opinion that a power over exports might be more effectual, than that over imports, in obtaining beneficial treaties of commerce.''

" Mr. GERRY was strenuously opposed to the power over exports. It might be made use of to compel the States to comply with the will of the General Government, and to grant it any new power which might be demanded. We have given it more power already than we know how will be exercised. It will enable the General Government to oppress the States, as much as Ireland is oppressed by Great Britain.''

" Mr. FITZSIMONS would be against a tax on exports to be laid immediately ; but was for giving a power of laying a tax when a proper time may call for it. This would certainly be the case when America should become a manufacturing country.''

" COLONEL MASON. — If he were for reducing the States to mere corporations, as seemed to be the tendency of some arguments, he should be for subjecting their exports, as well as imports, to a power of general taxation. . . The eight Northern States have an interest different from the five Southern States ; and have, in one branch of the Legislature, thirty-six votes against twenty-nine ; and in the other, in the proportion of eight against five. The Southern States had, therefore, ground for their suspicion. The case of exports was not the same with that of imports. The latter were the same throughout the States ; the former, very different.''

" Mr. CLYMER remarked that every State might reason with regard to its particular productions in the same manner as the Southern States. The Middle States may apprehend an oppression of their wheat, flour, provisions, etc. ; and with more reason, as these articles were exposed to a competition in foreign markets, not incident to tobacco, rice, etc.''

" Mr MADISON, in order to require two-thirds of each House to tax exports, as a lesser evil than a total prohibition, moved to insert the words, ' unless by consent of two-thirds of the Legislature.' ''

" Mr. WILSON seconds ; and on this question, it passed in the negative, — Aye, five ; No, six ; Virginia, COLONEL MASON, MR. RANDOLPH, MR. BLAIR, No ; GENERAL WASHINGTON, MR. MADISON, Aye."

August 23d. — " The following clause in the Report of the Committee of eleven, being taken up, — ' To make laws for organizing, arming and disciplining the militia, and for governing such parts of them as may be employed in the service of the United States ; reserving to the States, respectively, the appointment of the officers, and authority of training the militia according to the discipline prescribed.' ''

" Mr. SHERMAN moved to strike out the last member, ' and authority of training, etc.' ''

"MR. KING, by way of explanation, said that, by *organizing*, the Committee meant proportioning the officers and men,—by *arming*, specifying the kind, size, and calibre of arms,—and, by *disciplining*, prescribing the manual exercise, evolutions, etc."

"MR. GERRY. — This power in the United States, as explained, is making the States drill-sergeants. He had as lief let the citizens of Massachusetts be disarmed, as to take the command from the State, and subject them to the General Legislature. It would be regarded as a system of despotism."

" MR. KING added to his former explanation, that *arming* . . included the authority to regulate the modes of furnishing, either by the militia themselves, the State Government, or the National Treasury; that *laws* for disciplining must involve penalties, and everything necessary for enforcing penalties."

" MR. DAYTON moved to postpone the paragraph."

" On the motion to postpone, — *Aye*, three ; *No*, eight."

" MR. ELLSWORTH and MR. SHERMAN moved to postpone the second clause."

" MR. LANGDON said he could not understand the jealousy expressed by some gentlemen. The General and State Governments were not enemies to each other, but different institutions for the good of the people of America. As one of the people he could say, the National Government is mine, the State Government is mine. In transferring power from one to the other, I only take out of my left hand what it cannot so well use, and put it into my right hand, where it can be better used."

" MR. GERRY thought it was rather taking out of the right hand, and putting it into the left. Will any man say that liberty will be as safe in the hands of eighty or an hundred men taken from the whole Continent, as in the hands of two or three hundred from a single State ? "

" GENERAL PINCKNEY preferred the clause reported by the Committee, extending the meaning of it to the case of fines, etc."

" MR. MADISON. — The primary object is, to secure an effectual discipline of the militia. This will no more be done, if left to the States separately, than the requisitions have been hitherto paid by them The States neglect their militia now, . . in like manner as the militia of a State would have been still more neglected than it has been, if each county had been independently charged with the care of its militia. The discipline of the militia is evidently a *national* concern, and ought to be provided for in the *national* Constitution."

" MR. L. MARTIN was confident that the States would never give up the power over the militia."

" MR RANDOLPH asked what danger there could be, that the militia would be brought into the field, and made to commit suicide on themselves. This is a power that cannot, from its nature, be abused ; unless, indeed, the whole mass should be corrupted. . . He urged this as an essential point : observing that the militia were everywhere neglected by the State Legislatures, the members of which courted popularity too much to enforce a proper discipline."

" On the question on the motion of MR. ELLSWORTH and MR. SHERMAN, — *Aye*, one ; *No*, ten."

" On the question to agree to the first part of the clause, — ' To make laws for organizing, arming and disciplining the militia, and for governing such part of them as may be employed in the service of the United States,' — *Aye*, nine ; _ _ *No*, two."

" Mr. MADISON moved to amend the next part of the clause so as to read, 'reserving to the States, respectively, the appointment of the officers, *under the rank of general officers.*' "

·' Mr. SHERMAN considered this as absolutely inadmissible."

" Mr. GERRY. — Let us at once destroy the State Governments, have an Executive for life or hereditary, and a proper Senate ; and then there would be some consistency in giving full power to the General Government. . . He warned the Convention against pushing the experiment too far. Some people will support a plan of vigorous government at every risk. Others, of a more democratic cast, will oppose it with equal determination ; and a civil war may be produced by the conflict."

" Mr. MADISON. — As the greatest danger is that of disunion of the States, it is necessary to guard against it by sufficient powers to the common Government ; and as the greatest danger to liberty is from large standing armies, it is best to prevent them by an effectual provision for a good militia."

" On the question to agree to Mr. MADISON'S motion, — *Aye*, three ; *No*, eight."

" On the clause, 'and the authority of training the militia according to the discipline prescribed by the United States,' — *Aye*, seven ; *No*, four."

" Mr. RUTLEDGE moved to amend Article VIII. [in the Report of August 6th, p. 49], to read as follows : — ' This Constitution, and the laws of the United States made in pursuance thereof, and all the treaties made under the authority of the United States, shall be the supreme law of the several States and of their citizens and inhabitants ; and the Judges of the several States shall be bound thereby in their decisions, anything in the Constitution or laws of the several States to the contrary, notwithstanding,' — which was agreed, to *nem. con.*"

" Mr. GOUVERNEUR MORRIS moved to alter the first part of the clause [concerning the militia], so as to read, ' to provide for calling forth the militia, to execute the laws of the Union, suppress insurrections, and repel invasions ' — which was agreed to, *nem. con.*"

" Mr. CHARLES PINCKNEY moved, as an additional power to be vested in the Legislature of the United States, ' to negative all laws passed by the several States interfering, in the opinion of the Legislature, with the general interests and harmony of the Union ; provided that two-thirds of the members of each House assent to the same.' This principle, he observed, had formerly been agreed to. He considered the precaution as essentially necessary."

" MR. BROOM seconded the proposition."

" MR. MADISON proposed that it should be committed. He had been from the beginning a friend to the principle ; but thought the modification might be made better."

" MR. WILSON considered this as the key-stone wanted to complete the wide arch of government we are raising. The power of self-defence had been urged as necessary for the State Governments. It was equally necessary for the General Government. The firmness of Judges is not of itself sufficient. Something further is requisite. It will be better to prevent the passage of an improper law, than to declare it void when passed."

" MR. ELLSWORTH observed, that the power contended for would require that all laws of the State Legislatures should   .   .   be transmitted to the General Legislature, or that the State Executives should be appointed by the General Government, and have a control over the State laws."

" MR. PINCKNEY declared, that the State Executives ought to be so appointed, with such control ; and that it would be so provided, if another Convention should take place."

" MR. LANGDON was in favor of the proposition. He considered it as resolvable into the question, whether the extent of the National Constitution was to be judged of by the General or State Governments ?" *

" On the question for commitment, — *Aye*, five ; *No*, six."

August 25th. — " MR. MCHENRY and GENERAL PINCKNEY made the following proposition : — ' All duties, imposts and excises, prohibitions or restraints, laid or made by the Legislature of the United States, shall be uniform and equal throughout the United States.' "

" Referred [with other propositions], *nem. con.*, to a Committee composed of a member from each State."

August 28th. — The clause, — " No State, without the consent of the Legislature of the United States, shall lay impost or duties on imports," — being under consideration, —

" MR. KING moved to add, ' a prohibition on the States to interfere in private contracts.' "

" MR. GOUVERNEUR MORRIS. — This would be going too far."

" MR. WILSON was in favor of MR. KING's motion."

" MR. MADISON admitted that inconveniences might arise from such a prohibition ; but thought on the whole it would be overbalanced by the utility of it. He conceived, however, that a negative on the State laws could alone secure the effect." *

" COLONEL MASON observed, that particular States might wish to encourage, by impost duties, certain manufactures, for which they enjoyed natural advantages ; as Virginia, the manufacture of hemp, etc."

" MR. MADISON. — The encouragement of manufactures in that mode requires duties, not only on imports directly from foreign countries, but from the other States in the Union ; which would revive all the mischiefs experienced from the want of a General Government over commerce."

---

* Relative to the proposition for such a power, and the debates upon it, see pp. 16, 40.

" Mr. King moved to insert, after the word ' imports,' the words, ' or exports ;' so as to prohibit the States from taxing either."

" On the question, — *Aye*, six ; *No*, five."

August 30*th.* — The Article, — " The United States shall guaranty to each State a republican form of government ; and shall protect each State against invasions ; and, on the application of its Legislature, against domestic violence," — being taken under consideration, —

" Mr. Dickinson moved to strike out, ' on the application of its Legislature.' He thought it of essential importance to the tranquillity of the United States, that they should, in all cases, suppress domestic violence, which may proceed from the State Legislature itself, or from disputes between the two branches, where such may exist."

" On the question,—*Aye*, three ; *No*, eight."

" Mr. Dickinson moved to insert the words, ' or Executive,' after the words, ' application of its Legislature.' The occasion itself, he remarked, might hinder the Legislature from meeting."

" On this question, — *Aye*, eight; *No*, two ; Maryland, divided."

" Mr. L. Martin moved to subjoin to the last amendment, the words, ' in the recess of the Legislature,' — on which question, Maryland only, *Aye*."

" On the last clause as amended, — *Aye*, nine ; *No*, two."

The Article, — " The ratification of the Conventions of —— States shall be sufficient for organizing this Constitution."

" Mr. Sherman observed that the States being now confederated by Articles which require unanimity in changes, he thought the ratification, in this case, of ten States at least ought to be made necessary."

" Mr. Randolph was for filling the blank with ' nine,' that being a respectable majority of the whole, and being a number made familiar by the constitution of the existing Congress."

" Mr. Dickinson asked, whether the concurrence of Congress is to be essential to the establishment of the system—whether the refusing States in the Confederacy could be deserted—and whether Congress could concur in contravening the system under which they acted?"

" Mr. Wilson. — As the Constitution stands, the States only which ratify can be bound. We must, he said, in this case, go to the original powers of society. The house on fire must be extinguished, without a scrupulous regard to ordinary rights."

" Mr. Butler was in favor of ' nine.' He revolted at the idea that one or two States should restrain the rest from consulting their safety."

" Mr. King thought the amendment necessary ; otherwise, as the Constitution now stands, it will operate on the whole, though ratified by a part only."

August 31*st.* — " Mr. King moved to add to the end of the Article, the words, ' between the said States,' so as to confine the operation of the Government to the States ratifying it."

" On the question, — *Aye*, nine ; *No*, one."

" Mr. Sherman doubted the propriety of authorizing less than all the States to execute the Constitution, considering the nature of the existing Confederation."

" Mr. Carroll mentioned the mode of altering the Constitution of Maryland pointed out therein, and that no other mode could be pursued in tha: State."

" Mr. King.— . . Conventions alone, which will avoid all the obstacles from the complicated formation of the Legislatures, will succeed ; and, if not positively required by the plan, its enemies will oppose that mode."

" Mr. Madison considered it best to require Conventions. . . The difficulty in Maryland was no greater than in other States, where no mode of change was pointed out by their Constitution, and all officers were under oath to support it, The people were, in fact, the fountain of all power, and by recurring to them, all difficulties were got over They could alter constitutions as they pleased. It was a principle in the Bills of Rights, that first principles might be resorted to."   ·

" Mr. Gorham urged the expediency of Conventions ; also Mr. Pinckney, for reasons formerly urged on a discussion of this question."

" Mr. L. Martin insisted on a reference to the State Legislatures. He urged the danger of commotions from a resort to the people and to first principles ; in which the Government might be on one side, and the people on the other."

After the successive motions, to fill the blank with thirteen, ten, etc., had been negatived, " Colonel Mason [remarked that] nine States had been required in all great cases under the Confederation, and that number was on that account, preferable."

On the question for " nine," — *Aye*, eight ; *No*, three.

The Article, as amended, was then agreed to by all the States, Maryland excepted " [though Mr. Jenifer, one of its delegates, voted *Aye*]."

" On the question on the clause of the Report, — ' and all duties, imposts, and excises, laid by the Legislature, shall be uniform throughout the United States,' — it was agreed to, *nem. con.*"

The Article, as amended on motion of Mr. Gouverneur Morris and Mr. Pinckney, was then taken up ; viz. : — " This Constitution shall be laid before the United States in Congress assembled ; and it is the opinion of this Convention that it should afterwards be submitted to a Convention chosen in each State, in order to receive the ratification of such Conventions, to which end the several Legislatures ought to provide for the calling of Conventions within their respective States, as speedily as circumstances will permit."

" Mr. Gouverneur Morris said his object was, to impress in stronger terms the necessity of calling Conventions in order to prevent enemies to the plan from giving it the go-by. When it first appears, with the sanction of this Convention, the people will be favorable to it. By degrees the

State officers, and those interested in the State Governments, will intrigue, and turn the popular current against it."

" Mr. L. Martin believed Mr. Morris to be right, that after a while the people would be against it ; but for a different reason from that alleged. He believed they would not ratify it, unless hurried into it by surprise."

" Mr. Gerry enlarged on the idea of Mr. L. Martin, in which he concurred ; represented the system as full of vices ; and dwelt on the impropriety of destroying the existing Confederation, without the unanimous consent of the parties to it."

" Mr. Gerry moved to postpone the Article."

" Colonel Mason seconded the motion, declaring that he would sooner chop off his right hand, than put it to the Constitution as it now stands. He wished to see some points, not yet decided, brought to a decision. . . Should these points be improperly settled, his wish would then be, to bring the whole subject before another General Convention."

" Mr. Gouverneur Morris was ready for a postponement. He had long wished for another Convention, that will have the firmness to provide a vigorous Government, which we are afraid to do."

" On the question for postponing, — *Aye*, three ; *No*, eight."

" On the question on the Article, — *Aye*, ten ; Maryland, *No*."

September 5th. — The proposition, in the Report of the Committee of eleven, — " To add to the clause, ' to raise and support armies,' the words, ' but no appropriation of money for that use shall be for a longer term than two years,' " —being taken up, —

" Mr. Gerry objected, that it admitted of appropriations to an army for two years, instead of one ; for which he could not conceive a reason ; that it implied there was no a standing army, which he inveighed against, as dangerous to liberty — as unnecessary, even for so great an extent of country as this — and if necessary, some restriction on the number and duration ought to be provided. Nor was this a proper time for such an innovation. The people would not bear it."

" Mr. Sherman remarked, that the appropriations were *permitted* only, *not required*, to be for two years. As the Legislature is to be biennially elected, it would be inconvenient to require appropriations to be for one year, as there might be no session within the time necessary to renew them."

" The clause was then agreed to, *nem. con.*"

" The part of the clause, in the same Report, — ' to exercise like authority [exclusive legislation] over all places purchased for the erection of forts, magazines, arsenals, dock-yards, and other needful buildings,' — coming under consideration, — "

" Mr. Gerry contended that this power might be made use of to enslave any particular State, by buying up its territory, and that the strong-holds proposed would be a means of awing the State into an undue obedience to the General Government."

" Mr. King . . would move to insert, after the word ' purchased,' the words, ' by the consent of the Legislature of the State.' This would certainly make the power safe."

"Mr. Gouverneur Morris seconded the motion, which was agreed to *nem. con.*; as was then the residue of the clause, as amended."

September 7th. — The Section, — " The Vice-President shall be *ex-officio* President of the Senate," — being considered, —

"Mr. Gerry opposed this regulation. We might as well put the President himself at the head of the Legislature. The close intimacy that must subsist between the President and Vice-President makes it absolutely improper. He was against having any Vice-President."

"Mr. Gouverneur Morris. — The Vice-President then will be the first heir-apparent that ever loved his father. If there should be no Vice-President, the President of the Senate would be temporary successor, which would amount to the same thing."

"Mr. Sherman saw no danger in the case. If the Vice-President was not to be President of the Senate, . . some member, by being made President, must be deprived of his vote, unless when an equal division of votes might happen in the Senate, which would be but seldom."

"Mr. Randolph concurred in the opposition to the clause."

"Colonel Mason thought the office of Vice-President an encroachment on the rights of the Senate, and that it mixed too much the Legislative and the Executive, which, as well as the Judiciary department, ought to be kept as separate as possible."

" On the question, 'Shall the Vice-President be *ex-officio* President of the Senate ?' — *Aye*, eight ; *No*, two."

September 8th. — " Mr. McHenry observed, that the President had not yet been any where authorized to convene the Senate, and moved to amend Article VI., Section 2, by striking out the words, 'He may convene the Legislature on extraordinary occasions,' and inserting, 'He may convene both, or either of the Houses, on extraordinary occasions.'"

On the question, — *Aye*, seven ; *No*, four.

" A Committee was then appointed by ballot, to revise the style of, and arrange, the Articles which had been agreed to by the House. The Committee consisted of Mr. Johnson, Mr. Hamilton, Mr. Gouverneur Morris, Mr. Madison, and Mr. King."

"Mr. Williamson moved that, previous to this work of the Committee, the clause relating to the number of the House of Representatives should be reconsidered, for the purpose of increasing the number."

"Mr. Madison seconded the motion."

"Mr. Sherman opposed it. He thought the provision on that subject amply sufficient."

"Colonel Hamilton expressed himself with great earnestness and anxiety in favor of the motion. He avowed himself a friend to a vigorous government, but would declare, at the same time, he held it essential that the popular branch of it should be on a broad foundation. He was seriously of opinion, that the House of Representatives was on so narrow a scale, as to be really dangerous, and to warrant a jealousy in the people, for their liberties."

" On this motion to reconsider, — *Aye,* five ; *No,* six."

September 10*th.* — " MR. GERRY moved to reconsider the Article, — ' On the application of the Legislatures of two-thirds of the States in the Union, for an amendment of this Constitution, the Legislature of the United States shall call a Convention for that purpose.' "

This Constitution, he said, is to be paramount to the State Constitutions. It follows, hence, from this article, that two-thirds of the States may obtain a Convention, a majority of which can bind the Union to innovations that may subvert the State Constitutions altogether. He asked whether this was a situation proper to be run into ?

COLONEL HAMILTON seconded the motion ; but, he said, with a different view from Mr. GERRY. He did not object to the consequences stated by MR. GERRY. There was no greater evil in subjecting the people of the United States to the major voice, than the people of a particular State. It had been wished by many, and was much to have been desired, that an easier mode of introducing amendments had been provided by the Articles of Confederation. It was equally desirable now, that an easy mode should be established for supplying defects which will probably appear in the new system. The mode proposed was not adequate. The State Legislatures will not apply for alterations ; but with a view to increase their own powers. The National Legislature will be the first to perceive, and will be the most sensible to, the necessity of amendments ; and ought also to be empowered, whenever two-thirds of each branch should concur, to call a Convention. There could be no danger in giving this power, as the people would finally decide in the case.

" On MR. GERRY'S motion to reconsider, — *Aye,* nine ; *No,* one."

MR. SHERMAN moved to add to the article, " or the Legislature may propose amendments to the several States ; but no amendments shall be binding until consented to by the several States."

" MR. GERRY seconded the motion."

MR. MADISON moved to postpone the consideration of the proposition, in order to take up the following : —

" The Legislature of the United States, whenever two-thirds of both Houses shall deem necessary, or on application of two-thirds of the Legislatures of the several States, shall propose amendments to this Constitution, which shall be valid to all intents and purposes as part thereof, when the same shall have been ratified by three-fourths, at least, of the Legislatures of the several States, or by Conventions in three-fourths thereof, as one or the other mode of ratification may be proposed by the Legislature of the United States."

" COLONEL HAMILTON seconded the motion."

" The postponement being agreed to," —

" On the proposition of MR. MADISON and COLONEL HAMILTON," with the addition of the proviso offered by MR. RUTLEDGE, — *Aye,* nine ; *No,* one.*

* The proviso is contained in the 9th Section of the first Article in the Constitution.

"Mr. Pinckney moved, that it be an instruction to the Committee for r vising the style and arrangement of the Articles agreed on, to prepare an address to the people, to accompany the present Constitution, and to be laid, with the same, before the United States in Congress."

"The motion itself was referred to the Committee, *nem. con.*"

September 12th. — "Doctor Johnson, from the Committee of style, etc., reported a digest of the plan, of which printed copies were ordered to be furnished to the members. He also reported a letter to accompany the plan to Congress."

"The clause relating to exports being reconsidered at the instance of Colonel Mason, —

"He moved as follows : — ' provided nothing herein contained shall be construed to restrain any State from laying duties on exports for the sole purpose of defraying the charges of inspecting, packing, storing, and indemnifying the losses in keeping the commodities in the care of public officers, before exportation.' "

"Mr. Madison seconded the motion."

"Mr. Gorham and Mr. Langdon thought there would be no security, if the proviso should be agreed to, for the States exporting through other States, against the oppressions of the latter. How was redress to be obtained, in case duties should be laid beyond the purpose expressed ?"

"Mr. Madison.—There will be the same security as in other cases. The jurisdiction of the Supreme Court must be the source of redress. So far only had provision been made by the plan, against injurious acts of the States. His own opinion was, that this was insufficient. A negative on the State laws alone could meet all the shapes which these could assume. But this had been overruled." *

September 15th. — "Mr. Randolph animadverting on the indefinite and dangerous power given by the Constitution to Congress. expressing the pain he felt at differing from the body of the Convention on the close of the great and awful subject of their labors, . . . and anxiously wishing for some accommodating expedient which would relieve him from his embarrassments, made a motion importing, ' that amendments to the plan might be offered by the State Conventions, which should be submitted to, and finally decided on, by another general Convention.' Should this proposition be disregarded, it would, he said, be impossible for him to put his name to the instrument."

"Colonel Mason seconded and followed Mr. Randolph in animadversions on the dangerous power and structure of the Government, concluding that it would end either in monarchy, or a tyrannical aristocracy. . . This Constitution had been formed without the knowledge or idea of the pe pl . A second Convention will know more of the sense of the people. . . As the Constitution now stands, he could neither give it his support or vote in Virginia ; and he could not sign here what he could not support there. With the expedient of another Convention, as proposed, he could sign."

"Mr. Pinckney. — These declarations from members so respectable, at the close of this important scene, give a peculiar solemnity to the present moment. . . Nothing but confusion and contrariety will spring from the experiment [proposed]. He was not without objections, as well as others, to the plan. . . But apprehending the danger of a general confusion, and an ultimate decision by the sword, he should give the plan his support."

* See Mr. Madison's expressions as to such a power, on pp. 16, 40, 58

" Mr. GERRY stated the objections which determined him to withhold
his name from the Constitution. . . . .
" He could, however, he said, get over all these, if the rights of the citizens
were not rendered insecure. — first, by the general power of the Legislature to make what laws they may please to call ' necessary and proper ;'
secondly, to raise armies and money without limit ; thirdly, to establish a
tribunal without juries, which will be a Star Chamber as to civil cases.
Under such a view of the Constitution, the best that could be done, he
conceived, was to provide for a second General Convention."

" On the question, on the proposition of MR. RANDOLPH, all
the States answered, — *No.*"

" On the question, to agree to the Constitution as amended,
all the States, — *Aye.*"

" The Constitution was then ordered to be engrossed, and
the House Adjourned."

" MONDAY, *September 17th.*"

" The engrossed Constitution being read, —

" DOCTOR FRANKLIN rose to offer a speech which he had prepared in
writing for the occasion, and which MR. WILSON read, as follows : —

" MR. PRESIDENT,—

" I confess that there are several parts of this Constitution which I do
not at present approve, but I am not sure I never shall approve them.
For, having lived long, I have experienced many instances of being
obliged, by better information, or fuller consideration, to change opinions,
even on important subjects, which I once thought right, but found to be
otherwise. It is therefore that the older I grow, the more apt I am to
doubt my own judgment, and to pay more respect to the judgment of
others. . . . . In these sentiments, sir, I agree to
this Constitution, with all its faults, if they are such, because I think a
General Government necessary for us. . . . . I doubt too
whether any other Convention we can obtain may be able to make a better
Constitution. . . . . Thus I consent, sir,
to this Constitution, because I expect no better, and because I am not
sure that it is not the best. The opinions I have had of its errors I sacrifice
to the public good. I have never whispered a syllable of them abroad.
Within these walls they were born, and here they shall die. If every one
of us, in returning to our constituents, were to report the objections he has
had to it, and endeavor to gain partisans in support of them, we might .
prevent its being generally received ; and thereby lose all the salutary
effects and great advantages resulting naturally in our favor among foreign
nations. as well as among ourselves, from our real or apparent unanimity.
. . . I hope, therefore, that for our own sakes, as a part of the people,
and for the sake of posterity, we shall act heartily and unanimously in
recommending the Constitution (if approved by Congress and confirmed
by the Conventions) wherever our influence may extend ; and turn our
future thoughts and endeavors to the means of having it well administered.
" On the whole, sir, I cannot help expressing a wish that every member
of the Convention, who may still have objections to it, would with me, on
this occasion, doubt a little of his own infallibility, and, to make manifest
our unanimity. put his name to this instrument.''

" He then . . offered the following as a convenient form,
for signing ; viz. : — ' Done in Convention by the unanimous
consent of *the States* present, the seventeenth of September,

etc. In witness whereof we have hereunto subscribed our
names.' "

MR. MADISON states that, "This ambiguous form had been
drawn up by MR. GOUVERNEUR MORRIS, in order to gain the
dissenting members, and put into the hands of DOCTOR
FRANKLIN, that it might have the better chance of success."

" MR. GORHAM said, if not too late, he could wish, for the purpose of
lessening objections to the Constitution, that the clause, declaring that the
' number of Representatives shall not exceed one for every forty thousand,'
which had produced so much discussion, might be yet reconsidered, in
order to strike out ' forty thousand,' and insert ' thirty thousand.' This
would not, he remarked, establish that as an absolute rule, but only give
Congress a greater latitude, which could not be thought unreasonable."

" MR. KING and MR. CARROLL seconded and supported the ideas of
MR. GORHAM."

" When the President rose for the purpose of putting the question, he
said that, although his situation had hitherto restrained him from offering
his sentiments on questions depending in the House, and, it might be
thought, ought now to impose silence on him, yet he could not forbear
expressing his wish that the alteration proposed might take place. It was
much to be desired, that the objections to the plan recommended might be
made as few us possible. The smallness of the proportion of Representatives
had been considered, by many members of the Convention, an insufficient
security for the rights and interests of the people. He acknowledged that
it had always appeared to himself among the exceptionable parts of the
plan ; and late as the present moment was for admitting amendments, he
thought this of so much consequence, that it would give him much satisfaction to see it adopted." *

"No opposition was made to the proposition of MR.
GORHAM, and it was agreed to unanimously."

" On the question to agree to the Constitution, enrolled, in
order to be signed, it was agreed to, all the *States* answering,
Aye."

" MR. RANDOLPH then rose, and . . apologized for his refusing to
sign the Constitution, notwithstanding the vast majority and venerable
names that would give sanction to its wisdom and its worth. He said,
however, that he did not mean by this refusal to decide that he should
oppose the Constitution without-doors. He meant only to keep himself
free to be governed by his duty, as it should be prescribed by his future
judgment. He refused to sign, because he thought the object of the
Convention would be frustrated by the alternative which it presented to
the people. Nine States will fail to ratify the plan, and confusion must
ensue."

" MR. GOUVERNEUR MORRIS said, that he too had objections, but, considering the present plan as the best that was to be attained, he should take
it with all its faults. The majority had determined in its favor, and by
that determination he should abide. The moment this plan goes forth, all
other considerations will be laid aside, and the great question will be, —
Shall there be a National Government or not ? and this must take place,
or a general anarchy will be the alternative. He remarked that the signing,
in the form proposed, related only to the fact that *the States* present were
unanimous."

* MR. MADISON says, in a note, "This was the only occasion on which the President
entered at all into the discussions of the Convention."

" Mr. WILLIAMSON. — . . For himself he did not think a better plan was to be expected, and had no scruples against putting his name to it.''

" COLONEL HAMILTON expressed his anxiety that every member should sign. A few characters of consequence, by opposing, or even refusing to sign, the Constitution, might do infinite mischief, by kindling the latent sparks that lurk under an enthusiasm in favor of the Convention, which may soon subside. No man's ideas were more remote from the plan than his were known to be; but is it possible to deliberate between anarchy and convulsion on one side, and the chance of good to be expected from the plan on the other?''

'' Mr. BLOUNT said, he had declared that he would not sign so as to pledge himself in support of the plan, but he was relieved by the form proposed, and would, without committing himself, attest the fact that the plan was the unanimous act of the States in Convention.'' *

" Mr. RANDOLPH could not but regard the signing in the proposed form, as the same with signing the Constitution. The change of form, therefore, could make no difference with him. . . . He repeated his persuasion, that the holding out this plan, with a final alternative to the people of accepting or rejecting it *in toto*, would really produce the anarchy and civil convulsions which were apprehended from the refusal of individuals to sign it.''

" Mr. GERRY. — . . Whilst the plan was depending, he had treated it with all the freedom he thought it deserved. He now felt himself bound, as he was disposed, to treat it with the respect due to the act of the Convention. He hoped he should not violate that respect in declaring, on this occasion, his fears that a civil war may result from the present crisis of the United States. In Massachusetts, particularly, he saw the danger of this calamitous event. In that State there are two parties, one devoted to Democracy, the worst, he thought, of all political evils ; the other, as violent in the opposite extreme. From the collision of these, in opposing and resisting the Constitution, confusion was greatly to be feared. He had thought it necessary, for this and other reasons, that the plan should have been proposed in a more mediating shape, in order to abate the heat and opposition of parties. As it had been passed by the Convention, he was persuaded it would have the contrary effect He could not, therefore, by signing the Constitution, pledge himself to abide by it at all events. The proposed form made no difference with him.''

" GENERAL PINCKNEY. — We are not likely to gain many converts by the ambiguity of the proposed form of signing. He thought it best to be candid, and let the form speak the substance. If the meaning of the signers be left in doubt, his purpose would not be answered. He should sign the Constitution with a view to support it with all his influence, and wished to pledge himself accordingly.''

" Mr. INGERSOLL did not consider the signing, either as a mere attestation of the fact, or as pledging the signers to support the Constitution at all events ; but as a recommendation of what, all things considered, was the most eligible.''

" Mr. KING suggested that the Journals of the Convention should be either destroyed, or deposited in the custody of the President. He thought, if suffered to be made public, a bad use would be made of them by those who would wish to prevent the adoption of the Constitution.''

" Mr. WILSON preferred the second expedient. He had at one time liked the first best ; but, as false suggestions may be propagated, it should not be made impossible to contradict them.''

* MR. WILLIAM BLOUNT, from North Carolina. He took his seat in the Convention, *June 20th.*

" A question was then put on depositing the Journals, and other papers of the Convention, in the hands of the President; on which, — *Aye*, ten ; *No*, one."

"It was resolved, *nem. con.*, 'that he retain the Journal and other papers, subject to the order of Congress, if ever formed under the Constitution.'"

" The members then proceeded to sign the Constitution."

What those signers meant and understood to be the distinctive nature, and what the specific objects and purposes contemplated, they most explicitly declared in the following first clause of the Instrument : —

" WE, THE PEOPLE [not of the several States, but] OF THE UNITED STATES, in order to form a more perfect Union, establish justice, insure domestic tranquillity, provide for the common defence, promote the general welfare, and secure the blessings of liberty to ourselves and our posterity, do ordain and establish this Constitution for the United States of America."

In perfect harmony with the foregoing first clause, are the following extracts from the address or letter which, as proposed, Sept. 10th, was sent with the Constitution to Congress.

" SEPTEMBER 17*th*, 1787."

' We have now the honor to submit to the consideration of the United States in Congress assembled, that Constitution which has appeared to us the most advisable.

"In all our deliberations on this subject, we kept steadily in our view, that which appears to us the greatest interest of every true American,—the consolidation of our Union; in which is involved our prosperity, felicity, safety, perhaps our *national* existence.

" That it may promote the lasting welfare of that country so dear to us all, and secure her freedom and happiness, is our most ardent wish.

" With great respect, etc.,
" GEORGE WASHINGTON, *President.*"

" By unanimous order of the Convention."

As MR. MADISON relates, — " The Constitution being signed by all the members, except MR. RANDOLPH, MR. MASON, and MR. GERRY, who declined giving it the sanction of their names, the Convention dissolved itself by an adjournment *sine die.*"

" Whilst the last members were signing, DOCTOR FRANKLIN, looking towards the President's chair, at the back of which a rising sun happen d to be painted, observed to a few members near him, that painters had found it difficult to distinguish in their art, a rising, from a setting sun. I have, said he, often and often, in the course of the session, an t the vicissitudes of my hopes and fears as to its issue, looked at that behind the President, without being able to tell whether it was rising or setting ; but now, at length, I have the happiness to know, that it is *a rising* and *not a setting* sun."

Such was the progress, and such the conclusion, of the difficult and vastly momentous labors of the Convention of — — 1787, — labors, which ought to be far better understood, so that if possible they may be justly appreciated by every , American citizen, whether native or adopted.

It is suggested, as a matter of much interest and consequence, to notice the modifying effects of the influences exerted by some of the members, of broadest and maturest experience; of most cultivated, enlarged, and comprehensive patriotism ; as those effects are apparent from the beginning till the full attainment of that auspicious result, which had been long hoped for, with manifestly anxious and tremulous doubt, — whether hard-earned Independence was to run riot in lawless anarchy ; or whether dear-bought Liberty was to be regulated and secured by the operations of a well-organized and adequately efficient government.

As the Achievement of independence gave to the Declaration its reputed importance; so, the Construction of the government by that Convention gave to both of them, their practical value and significance.

The portion of the debates relating to slavery, have been purposely omitted ; because the final abolition of it seems to have superseded the expediency of further controversy or agitation on the subject. Besides, it appeared to be inconsistent with the main design, to introduce a subject likely to divert attention from that continued line of division, which so clearly marked the whole proceedings of the Convention, which has been mentioned or alluded to in these pages as deranging and endangering the plans of public operations from an early stage of the Revolution, and which, on that floor, as has been shown, more than once threatened to entirely defeat the best-directed, the most strenuous and ablest, efforts to remedy the rapidly increasing complication of appalling evils, then prevailing throughout the length and breadth of the country.

Nor did that division end with the process of forming the Constitution.

But it continued still so unabated, that, during the interval of suspense which followed, labors no less difficult and anxious than in its formation, were required and effectively performed to procure its acceptance.

Moreover, decidedly opposite opinions of its character and tendencies were as emphatically declared by some prominent men outside of the Convention, as such opinions were declared by some of the members inside of that justly venerated Assembly.

These facts would seem to need for confirmation, no plainer evidence than the immediately following extracts.

GENERAL WASHINGTON, to DAVID STEWART. — Mount Vernon, *Oct.* 17, 1787. "Dear Sir, — As the enclosed *Advertiser* contains a speech of MR. WILSON's, as able, candid, and honest a member as was in the Convention, which will place the most of COLONEL MASON's objections in their true point of light, I send it to you. The republication of it, if you can get it done, will be serviceable at this juncture."

SAME, to COLONEL HAMILTON, *Oct.* 18, 1787. — "It is with unfeigned concern I perceive a political dispute has arisen between GOVERNOR CLINTON and yourself. For both of you I have the highest esteem and regard. But, as you say it is insinuated by some of your political adversaries, and may obtain credit, 'that you *palmed* yourself upon me, and were *dismissed* from my family,' and call on me to do you justice by a recital of facts, I do therefore explicitly declare, that both charges are entirely unfounded. With respect to the first, I have no cause to believe that you ever took a single step to accomplish, or had the most distant idea of receiving, an appointment in my family, till you were invited into it; and, with respect to the second, your quitting it was altogether the effect of your own choice.

"When the situation of this country calls loudly for vigor and unanimity, it is to be lamented that gentlemen of talents and character should disagree in their sentiments for promoting the public weal ; but, unfortunately, this ever has been, and probably ever will be the case, in the affairs of mankind."

THOMAS JEFFERSON, to JOHN ADAMS,* Paris, *Nov.* 13, 1787. — "How do you like our new Constitution? I confess there are things in it, which stagger all my dispositions to subscribe to what such an Assembly has proposed. The House of federal Representatives will not be adequate to the management of affairs, either foreign or federal. Their President seems a bad edition of a Polish king. He may be elected from four years to four years, for life. Reason and experience prove to us, that a Chief Magistrate, so continuable, is an office for life. . . . Once in office, and possessing the military force of the Union, without the aid or check of a council, he would not be easily dethroned, even if the people could be induced to withdraw their votes from him. I wish that at the end of the four years, they had made him for ever ineligible a second time. Indeed, I think all the good of this new Constitution might have been couched in three or four new Articles, to be added to the good, old, and venerable fabric,† which should have been preserved, even as a religious relic."

GENERAL WASHINGTON, to BUSHROD WASHINGTON,‡ *Nov.* 10, 1787. — "The only question with me was, whether it [the Constitution] would go forth under favorable auspices, or receive the stamp of disapprobation. The opponents I expected (for it ever has been, that the adversaries of a measure are more active than its friends), would endeavor to stamp it with unfavorable impressions, in order to bias the judgment that is ultimately to decide upon it. This is evidently the case with the writers in opposition, whose objections are better calculated to alarm the fears, than to convince the judgment, of their readers. They build their objections upon principles that do not exist, which the Constitution does not support them in, and the existence of which has, by an appeal to the Constitution itself, been flatly denied ; and then, as if they were unanswerable, draw all the dreadful consequences that are necessary to alarm the apprehensions of the ignorant or unthinking. It is not the interest of the major part of these characters to be convinced ; nor will their *local* views yield to arguments

* Mr. Jefferson and Mr. Adams were American Ministers at foreign courts; the former, at that of France, the latter at the court of Great Britain.

† By " venerable fabric " Mr. Jefferson meant the Confederation.

‡ Afterwards Judge Washington, of the supreme court of the United States.

which do not accord with their present or future prospects. . . It is agreed on all hands, that no Government can be well administered without powers ; yet, the instant these are delegated, though those who are intrusted with the administration, are no more than the creatures of the people, act as it were but for a day, and are answerable for every step they take ; they are, from the moment they receive it, set down as tyrants. One would conceive from this, that their natures are immediately changed, and that they have no other disposition but to oppress. Of these things, in a government constituted and guarded as ours is, I have no idea, and do firmly believe that. whilst many ostensible reasons are assigned to prevent the adoption of it,' the real ones are concealed behind the curtain; because they are not of a nature to appear in open day. I believe further, supposing them pure, that evils as great result from too great jealousy, as from the want of it."

THOMAS JEFFERSON, to COLONEL SMITH,* *Nov.* 13, 1787. — "I do not know whether it is to yourself, or MR. ADAMS, I am to give my thanks for the copy of the new Constitution. I beg leave through you, to place them where due. . . . There are very good Articles in it, and very bad. I do not know which preponderate. . . . What we have always read of the elections of Polish Kings, should have forever excluded this idea of one continuable for life. . . . The British Ministry have so long hired their gazetteers to repeat, and model into every form, lies about our being in anarchy, that the world has at length believed them, . . . and what is more wonderful, we have believed them ourselves. Yet, where does this anarchy exist? Where did it ever exist. except in the single instance of Massachusetts? And can history produce an instance of rebellion so honorably conducted? I say nothing of its motives. . . . God forbid we should ever be twenty years without such a rebellion. . . . We have had thirteen States independent for eleven years. There has been one rebellion. That comes to one rebellion in a century and a half, for each State. . . . What country can preserve its liberties, if its rulers are not warned, from time to time, that this people preserve the spirit of resistance? Let them take arms. The remedy is, to set them right as to facts, pardon and pacify them. What signify a few lives lost in a century or two? The tree of liberty must be refreshed from time to time, with the blood of patriots and tyrants. It is its natural manure. Our Convention has been too much impressed by the insurrection of Massachusetts ; and, on the spur of the moment, they are setting up a kite to keep the hen-yard in order. I hope in God, this Article [relating to the office of President] will be rectified, before the new Constitution is accepted."

GENERAL WASHINGTON, to COLONEL HAMILTON. — *Nov.* 10, 1787. "Dear Sir, — I thank you for the pamphlet contained in your letter of the 30th ultimo. For the remaining numbers of PUBLIUS I shall acknowledge myself obliged, as I am persuaded the subject will be well handled by the author of them."

SAME, to DAVID STEWART, *Nov.* 30, 1787. — "I have seen no publication yet, that ought in my judgment to shake the proposed Constitution in the mind of an impartial and candid public. In fine, I have hardly seen one, that is not addressed to the passions of the people, and obviously calculated to alarm their fears. . . . That there are some writers, and others perhaps who have not written, that wish to see this Union divided into several Confederacies, is pretty evident. As an antidote to these opinions, and in order to investigate the ground of objections to the Constitution which is submitted, the *Federalist*, under the signature of PUBLIUS, is written. The numbers which have been published. I send you. If there. is a printer in Richmond, who is really well disposed to support

---

* Colonel Smith was Minister Adams's Secretary.

the new Constitution, he would do well to give them a place in his paper. They are, I think I may venture to say, written by able men ; and, before they are finished, will, or I am mistaken, place matters in a true point of light." *

THOMAS JEFFERSON, to WILLIAM CARMICHAEL, Dec. 11, 1787.—" MR. ADAMS, as you know, has asked his recall. This has been granted, and COLONEL SMITH is to return too.

"Our new Constitution is powerfully attacked in the American newspapers. The objections are, that its effect would be, to form the thirteen States into one ; that, proposing to melt all down into one General Government, they have fenced the people by no *Declaration of Rights* ; they have not renounced the power of keeping a standing army ; they have not secured the liberty of the press ; they have reserved the power of abolishing *Trials by Jury* in civil cases ; they have proposed that the laws of the Federal Legislature shall be paramount to the laws and constitutions of the States ; they have abandoned rotation in office ; and particularly, their President may be re-elected from four years to four years, for life, so as to render him a king for life, like a king of Poland : and they have not given him either the check or aid of a council. To these they add calculations of expense, etc.

"You will perceive that those objections are serious, and some of them not without foundation. The Constitution, however, has been received with very general enthusiasm, and as far as can be judged from external demonstrations, the bulk of the people are eager to adopt it. In the Eastern States, the printers will print nothing against it, unless the writer subscribes his name. . . . In New York, there is a division. The Governor (CLINTON) is known to be hostile to it.† . . . Pennsylvania is divided, and all the bitterness of her factions has been kindled anew on it. But the party in favor of it is strongest, both in and out of the Legislature. This is the party anciently of MORRIS, WILSON, etc. . . . As to Virginia, two of her Delegates refused to sign it. . . . Besides these, HENRY. HARRISON, NELSON, and the LEES are against it. GENERAL WASHINGTON will be for it, but it is not in his character to exert himself much in the case. MADISON will be its main pillar ; but it is questionable whether he can bear the weight of such a host. So that the presumption is, that Virginia will reject it. I know nothing of the dispositions of the States south of this. Should it fall through, as is possible, . . it is probable that Congress will propose that the objections being once known, another Convention shall be assembled. . . . In this way, union may be produced under a happy Constitution, and one which shall not be too energetic."

GENERAL WASHINGTON, to JAMES MADISON, in Congress, Dec. 7, 1787.— " MY DEAR SIR, — Since my last to you, I have been favored with your letters of the 28th of October and 18th of November. With the last came seven numbers of the *Federalist*, under the signature of PUBLIUS, for which I thank you. They are forwarded to a gentleman in Richmond for republication ; the doing of which in this State will, I am persuaded, have a good effect ; as there are certainly characters, who are no friends to a General Government. Perhaps I should not go too far, were I to add, who have no great objection to the introduction of anarchy and confusion.

" The solicitude to discover what the several State Legislatures would do with the Constitution, is now transferred to the several Conventions. . . . North Carolina, it has been said by some accounts from Richmond, will be governed in a great measure by the conduct of Virginia.

---

* Few, it is presumed, need to be told at this day, that these numbers were written by Alexander Hamilton, John Jay, and James Madison.

† See General Washington's letter, October 18, p. 70, in reply to one from Colonel Hamilton.

The pride of South Carolina will not, I conceive, suffer this influence to work in her councils; and the disturbances in Georgia will, or I am mistaken, show the people the propriety of being united, and the necessity there is for a General Government. If these, with the States eastward and northward of us, should accede to the Government, I think the citizens of this State will have no cause to bless the opponents of it here, if they should carry their point." *

THOMAS JEFFERSON, to JAMES MADISON, *Dec.* 20, 1787. — " I will now tell you what I do not like [in the proposed Constitution]. First, the omission of a *Bill of Rights.* . . . To say, as MR. WILSON does, that a *Bill of Rights* is not necessary, . . . is opposed by strong inferences from the body of the instrument, as well as from the omission of the clause of our present Confederation, which had made the reservation in express terms. Let me add, that a *Bill of Rights* is what the people are entitled to against every Government on earth, general and particular; and what no just Government should refuse or rest on inference.

" The second feature I dislike, and strongly dislike, is the abandonment in every instance, of the principle of rotation in office, and most particularly in the case of the President. Reason and experience tell us that the First Magistrate will always be re-elected, if he may be re-elected. He is then an officer for life. . . . Smaller objections are the appeals on matters of fact, as well as law; and the binding all persons, Legislative, Executive, and Judiciary, by oath, to maintain that Constitution. I do not pretend to decide what would be the best method of procuring . other good things in this Constitution, and of getting rid of the bad. Whether by adopting it, in hopes of future amendment ; or, after it shall have been duly canvassed by the people, . . . to say to them ; We see now what you wish. . . . Be it so. Send together your Deputies again. Let them establish your fundamental rights by a sacrosanct declaration, and let them pass the parts of the Constitution you have approved. These will give power to your Federal Government sufficient for your happiness.

" This is what might be said, and would probably produce a speedy, more perfect, and more permanent form of Government." †

GENERAL WASHINGTON, to the MARQUIS DE LAFAYETTE, *Feb.* 7, 1788. — You appear to be, as might be expected from a real friend to this country, anxiously concerned about its present political situation. . . . As to my sentiments with respect to the merits of the new Constitution, I will disclose them without reserve, although by passing through the post-offices they should become known to all the world ; for in truth, I have nothing to conceal on that subject.

It appears to me, then, little short of a miracle, that Delegates from so many States, different from each other, as you know, in their manners, circumstances, and prejudices, should unite in forming a system of National Government so little liable to well-founded objections. . . Nor yet am I such an enthusiastic, partial, or undiscriminating admirer of it

* *April 25th,* — GENERAL WASHINGTON wrote to JOHN ARMSTRONG — " Baffled in their attacks upon the Constitution, they have attempted to vilify and debase the characters who formed it; but even here I trust they will not succeed. Upon the whole, I doubt whether the opposition to the Constitution will not ultimately be productive of more good than evil. It has called forth in its defence abilities, which would not perhaps have otherwise existed. . . . It has given the rights of man a full and fair discussion, and explained in so clear and forcible a manner, as cannot fail to make a lasting impression upon those who read the last publications on the subject, and particularly the pieces under the signature of PUBLIUS. There will be a greater weight of abilities opposed to the System in the Convention of this State [Virginia], than there has been in any other."

† The next day, Dec. 21, Mr. Jefferson wrote to Colonel E. Carrington, — " As to the new Constitution, I find myself nearly a neutral; " and referred him to the explanation in the above letter to Mr. Madison.

as not to perceive it is tinctured with some real, though not radical, defects. . .   With regard to the two great points, the pivots upon which the whole machine must move, my creed is simply, —

" *First*, that the General Government is not invested with more powers than are indispensably necessary to perform the functions of a good government, and consequently no objection ought to be made against the quantity of power delegated to it.

Secondly, that these powers — as the appointment of all rulers will ever arise from, and at short stated intervals recur to, the free suffrage of the people — are so distributed among the Legislative, Executive, and Judicial branches, into which the General Government is arranged, that it can never be in danger of degenerating into a monarchy, an oligarchy, an aristocracy, or any other despotic or oppressive form, so long as there shall remain any virtue in the body of the people.

"I would not be understood, my dear Marquis, to speak of consequences which may be produced · in the revolution of ages, by corruption of morals, profligacy of manners, and listlessness in the preservation of the natural and inalienable rights of mankind, . . as these are contingencies against which no human prudence can effectually provide.

"It will at least be a recommendation to the proposed Constitution, that it is provided with more checks and barriers against the introduction of tyranny, and those of a nature less liable to be surmounted, than any government hitherto instituted among mortals. We are not to expect perfection in this world. . . Should that which is now offered to the people of America be found, on experiment, less perfect than it can be made, a constitutional door is left open for its amelioration.

" Some respectable characters have wished that the States, after having pointed out whatever alterations and amendments may be judged necessary, would appoint another Federal Convention to modify it upon those suggestions.   For myself, I have wondered that sensible men should not see the impracticability of this scheme.   The members would go fortified with such instructions that nothing but discordant ideas could prevail. Had I but slightly suspected, at the time when the late Convention was in session, that another Convention would not be likely to agree upon a better form of government, I should now be confirmed in the fixed belief that they would not be able to agree upon any system whatever; so many, I may add, such contradictory and unfounded objections have been urged against the system in contemplation, many of which would operate equally against any efficient government that might be proposed. I will only say, as a further opinion, founded on the maturest deliberation, that there is no alternative, no hope of alteration, no resting-place, between the adoption of this, and a recurrence to an unqualified state of anarchy, with all its deplorable consequences."

Thomas Jefferson, to A. Donald, *Feb.* 7, 1788. — " I wish, with all my soul, that the nine first conventions may accept the new Constitution. . . .   But I equally wish that the four latest conventions, whichever they be, may refuse to accede to it, till a *Declaration of Rights* be annexed. . .   By a *Declaration of Rights*, I mean one which shall stipulate freedom of religion, freedom of the press, freedom of commerce against monopolies, *Trial by Jury* in all cases, no suspension of the *habeas corpus, no standing armies.*   These are fetters against doing evil which no honest government should decline. There is another strong feature in the new Constitution, which I as strongly dislike ; that is *the perpetual re-eligibility of the President.* . It will be productive of cruel distress to our country, even in your day and mine."

General Washington, to the Marquis de Lafayette, *April* 28, 1788. — " At present, or under our existing form of Confederation, it would be idle to think of making commercial regulations on our part. One State passes a prohibitory law respecting some article ; another State opens wide the avenue for its admission. One Assembly makes a system,— another Assembly unmakes it. Virginia, in the very last session of her Legislature, was about to pass some of the most extravagant and preposterous edicts on the subject of trade that ever stained the leaves of a legislative code. It is in vain to hope for a remedy of these, and innumerable other evils, until a General Government shall be adopted.

"The Conventions of six States only have as yet accepted the new Constitution. No one has rejected it.

"On the general merits of this proposed Constitution I wrote to you some time ago my sentiments pretty freely.* . . . Although it is not to be expected that every individual in society will or can be brought to agree upon what is exactly the best form of government, yet there are many things in the Constitution which only need to be explained in order to prove equally satisfactory to all parties. For example, there was not a member of the Convention, I believe, who had the least objection to what is contended for by the advocates for a *Bill of Rights*, and *Trial by Jury*. The first, where the people evidently retained everything which they did not in express terms give up, was considered nugatory ; as you will find to have been more fully explained by Mr. Wilson and others ; and as to the second, it was only the difficulty of establishing a mode which should not interfere with the fixed modes of any of the States, that induced the Convention to leave it as a matter of future adjustment.

"There are other points on which opinions would be more likely to vary. As, for instance, on the *ineligibility of the* same person for *President*, after he should have served a certain course of years. Guarded so effectually as the proposed Constitution is, in respect to the prevention of bribery and undue influence in the choice of President, I confess I differ widely myself from MR. JEFFERSON and you, as to the expediency or necessity of rotation in that appointment. The matter was fairly discussed in the Convention, and to my full conviction ; though I cannot have time or room to sum up the arguments in this letter. There cannot, in my judgment, be the least danger that the President will, by any practicable intrigue, ever be able to continue himself one moment in office, much less to perpetuate himself in it, but in the last stage of corrupted morals and political depravity ; and even then, there is as much danger that any other species of domination would prevail. Though, when a people shall have become incapable of governing themselves, and fit for a master, it is of little consequence from what quarter he comes. Under an extended view of this part of the subject, I can see no propriety in precluding ourselves from the services of any man who, in some great emergency, shall be deemed universally most capable of serving the public." †

The Convention of New Hampshire adopted the Constitution, *June 21st*, and that of Virginia, *June 25th*.

As has been shown, the Constitution had at length been accepted and ratified by even a greater number of States than, by its provisions, were required to give it legitimate

---

* See the letter of February 7, p. 73.

† In a letter to Lafayette, *June 18th*, General Washington said :—"In a letter I wrote you a few days ago . . I gave you the state of politics to that period. Since which the Convention of South Carolina has ratified the Constitution by a great majority. That of this State has been sitting almost three weeks. . . It is probable the majority will be small, let it fall on whichever part it may. I am inclined to believe it will be in favor of the adoption. The Conventions of New York and New Hampshire both assemble this week. A large proportion of the members, with the Governor at their head, in the former, are said to be opposed to the Government in contemplation. New Hampshire, it is thought, will adopt it without much hesitation or delay. It is a little strange that the men of large property in the South should be more afraid that the Constitution will produce an aristocracy or a monarchy, than the genuine democratical people of the East. Such are our actual prospects. The accession of one State more will complete the number which by the constitutional provision will be sufficient, in the first instance, to carry the Government into effect."

force and effect. It was thus rendered the established and permanent form of Government, to be observed and obeyed throughout those States.

In reference to that exceedingly important event, and to other favorable indications about that time, GENERAL WASHINGTON, in a letter to GENERAL LINCOLN, *June 29th*, wrote : — " No one can rejoice more than I do, at every step the people of this great country take to preserve the Union, to establish good order and Government, and to render the Nation happy at home and respectable abroad. No country upon earth ever had it more in its power to attain these blessings than United America."

It may be seen, however, that the prospect, which appeared then so encouraging, was of short duration.

The indirect and secret course assumed by the opponents of the Constitution, soon excited anxiety and solicitude nearly or quite as intense as had been experienced before.

GENERAL WASHINGTON, to JAMES MCHENRY, *July 31st*, 1788. — " Dear Sir, — . . I am less likely than almost any person to have been informed of the circumstance to which you allude.* That some of the leading characters among the opponents of the proposed Government have not laid aside their ideas of obtaining great and essential changes, through a constitutional opposition, as they term it, may be collected from their public speeches. That others will use more secret and perhaps insidious means to prevent its organization, may be presumed from their previous conduct on the subject. . . The casual information received from visitants at my house would lead me to expect that a considerable effort will be made to procure the election of anti-federalists to the first Congress, in order to bring the subject immediately before the State Legislatures, to open an extensive correspondence between the minorities, for obtaining alterations, and, in short, to *undo* all that has been done.

" It is reported that a respectable neighbor of mine has said the Constitution cannot be carried into execution without great amendments. . . I think there will be great reason for those who are well affected to the Government, to use their utmost exertions that the worthiest citizens may be appointed to the two Houses of the first Congress. . . For much will doubtless depend on their prudence in conducting business at the beginning, and reconciling discordant dispositions to a reasonable acquiescence with candid and honest measures.

" I earnestly pray that the Omnipotent Being, who has not deserted the cause of America in the hour of its extremest hazard, may never yield so fair a heritage of freedom a prey to anarchy or despotism."

SAME, to GENERAL LINCOLN, *August 28th*, 1788. — " So far as I am able to learn, federal principles are gaining ground considerably. . . I will, however, just mention that there are suggestions that attempts will be made to procure the election of a number of anti-federal characters to the first Congress, in order to embarrass the details of Government, and produce premature alterations in its Constitution. . . It will be advisable, I should think, for the federalists to be on their guard, so far as not to suffer any secret machinations to prevail, without taking measures to frustrate them. . . I will confess, my apprehension is, that the New York circular letter is intended to bring on a General Convention at too early

---

* " A concerted and organized combination among those opposed to the Constitution, in different parts of the Union, with the view to suspend its operation, or defeat it altogether."

a period, and, in short, by referring the subject to the Legislatures, to set everything afloat again. I wish I may be mistaken, in imagining that there are persons who, upon finding they could not carry their point by an open attack upon the Constitution, have some sinister designs, to be silently effected, if possible. But I' trust in that Providence, which has saved us in six troubles, yea, in seven, to rescue us again from any imminent though unseen dangers. Nothing, however, on our part, ought to be left undone. I conceive it to be of unspeakable importance that whatever there be of wisdom and prudence and patriotism on the Continent, should be concentred in the public councils at the outset."

SAME, to COLONEL HAMILTON, *August* 28*th*, 1788. — "Dear Sir, — I have had the pleasure to receive your letter, dated the 13th, accompanied by one to GENERAL MORGAN. . . .

"As the perusal of the political papers under the signature of PUBLIUS has afforded me great satisfaction, I shall certainly consider them as claiming a most distinguished place in my library. I have read every performance which has been printed, on one side and the other of the great question lately agitated, so far as I have been able to obtain them ; and, without an unmeaning compliment, I will say, that I have seen no other so well calculated, in my judgment, to produce conviction on an unbiassed mind, as the production of your *triumvirate*. When the transient circumstances and fugitive performances which attended this crisis shall have disappeared, that work will merit the notice of posterity ; because in it are candidly and ably discussed the principles of freedom and the topics of Government, which will be always interesting to mankind so long as they shall be connected in civil society."

"The circular letter from your Convention, I presume, was the equivalent by which you obtained an acquiescence in the proposed Constitution. . . I am not very well satisfied with the tendency of it : yet the federal affairs have proceeded, with few exceptions, in so good a train, that I hope the political machine may be put in motion, without much effort or hazard of miscarrying.*

"On the delicate subject with which you conclude your letter I can say nothing, because the event alluded to may never happen, and because . . I would not wish to conceal my prevailing sentiment from you ; for you know me well enough, my good sir, to be persuaded that I am not guilty of affectation when I tell you, that it is my great and sole desire to live and die in peace and retirement on my own farm. . . Still I hope I shall always possess firmness and virtue enough to maintain what I consider the most enviable of titles, *the character of an honest man*, as well as prove what I desire to be considered in reality, that

I am, with great sincerity and esteem, dear sir, etc."†

GENERAL WASHINGTON, to THOMAS JEFFERSON, *Aug.* 31*st*, 1788. — "The merits and defects of the proposed Constitution have been largely and ably discussed. . . I can say there are scarcely any of the amendments which have been suggested to which I have much objection, except that

---

* Concerning the circular referred to, Mr. Madison wrote: — "You will have seen the circular letter from the Convention of this State [New York]. It has a pestilent tendency. If an early General Convention cannot be parried, it is seriously to be feared, that the System which has resisted so many direct attacks, may be at last successfully undermined by its enemies" — *New York, Aug.* 11*th*.
"This circular letter was sent by the Convention of New York to the Legislatures of the several States, recommending that a new General Convention should be called, for the purpose of taking into consideration various amendments to the Constitution. The Assembly of Virginia convened soon afterwards, and adopted strong Resolutions to the same effect. and sent an application to Congress, and a circular letter to the several States, recommending another General Convention."

† *From Colonel Hamilton's letter.* — "I take it for granted, sir, you have concluded to comply with what will undoubtedly be the general call of your country in relation to the new Government. You will permit me to say, that it is indispensable you should lend yourself to its first operations. It is to little purpose to have introduced a System, if the weightiest influence is not given to its firm establishment in the outset."— *Aug.* 13*th*.

which goes to the prevention of direct taxation. And that, I presume, will be more strenuously advocated and insisted upon hereafter than any other. I had indulged the expectation, that the new Government would enable those entrusted with its administration, to do justice to the public creditors and retrieve the national character. But if no means are to be employed but requisitions, that expectation was vain, and we may as well recur to the old Confederation. If the System can be put in operation without touching much the pockets of the people, perhaps it may be done; but, in my judgment, infinite circumspection and prudence are yet necessary in the experiment. It is nearly impossible for any one who has not been on the spot,* to conceive what the delicacy and danger of our situation have been. Though the peril is not past entirely, thank God, the prospect is somewhat brightening."

SAME, to HENRY LEE, in Congress, *Sept.* 22*d*, 1788. — "Your observations on the solemnity of the crisis and its application to myself, bring before me subjects of the most momentous and interesting nature.† In our endeavors to establish a new General Government, the contest, Nationally considered, seems not to have been so much for glory as [for] existence. It was for a long time doubtful whether we were to survive as an independent Republic, or decline from our federal dignity into insignificant and wretched fragments of an Empire. The adoption of the Constitution so extensively, and with so liberal an acquiescence on the part of the minorities in general, promised the former; until lately, the circular letter of New York, carried, in my apprehension, an unfavorable, if not an insidious tendency to a contrary policy. I still hope for the best; but before you mentioned it, I could not help fearing it would serve as a standard, to which the disaffected might resort. It is now evidently the part of all honest men, who are friends of the new Constitution, to endeavor to give it a chance to disclose its merits and defects, by carrying it fairly into effect in the first instance. For it is to be apprehended, that by an attempt to obtain amendments before the experiment has been fairly made, 'more is meant than meets the ear;' that an intention is concealed to accomplish slily what could not have been done openly, — *to undo all that has been done.*

If . . . a kind of combination is forming to stifle the Government in embryo, it is a happy circumstance that the design has become suspected. Preparations should be the sure attendant upon forewarning. Probably prudence, wisdom, and patriotism, were never more essentially necessary than at the present moment; and so far as it can be done in an irreproachably direct manner, no effort ought to be left unassayed to procure the election of the best possible characters to the new Congress. On their harmony, deliberation, and decision, everything will depend. . .

"The principal topic of your letter is to me a point of great delicacy indeed, insomuch that I can scarcely without impropriety touch upon it.†

---

* An expression he many times employed in the Revolutionary war, with reference to the pressing exigencies proceeding from a similar cause.

† *From Colonel Lee's letter.* — "My dear General, — At length the new Government has received the last act necessary to its existence. This day Congress passed the requisite previous arrangements. The first Wednesday in January the ratifying States are to appoint Electors; on the first Wednesday in February the President is to be chosen; and the first Wednesday in March is the time, and this city [New York] the place, for commencing proceedings. . . . . The solemnity of the moment, and its application to yourself, has fixed my mind in contemplations of a public and personal nature; and I feel an involuntary impulse which I cannot resist, of communicating without reserve to you some of the reflections which the hour has produced. Solicitous for our common happiness as a people, and convinced, as I continue to be, that our peace and prosperity depend on the proper improvement of the present period, my anxiety is extreme that the new Government may have an auspicious beginning. To effect this, and to perpetuate a Nation formed under your auspices, it is certain that again you will be called forth. . . The new Government . . must encounter . many difficulties. The obstacles to its harmonious progress will receive additional weight and influence from the active and enterprising characters, who continue to inflame the passions and systematize the measures of opposition. The circular letter from this State [New York], seems to be the standard to which the various minorities will repair : and, if they should succeed in bringing quickly into action the objects of that letter, new and serious difficulties must arise which will cross and may destroy the Government in its infancy." — *New York, Sept.* 10*th.*

. . You are among the small number of those who know my invincible
attachment to domestic life, and that my sincerest wish is, to continue in
the enjoyment of it solely until my final hour. . . Now justice to
myself and tranquillity of conscience require, that I should act a part, if
not above imputation, at least capable of vindication. . .

" While doing what my conscience informed me was right, as it respected my God, my country, and myself, I could despise all the party
clamor and unjust censure, which might be expected from some, whose
personal enmity might be occasioned by their hostility to the Government.
I am concious that I fear alone to give any real occasion for obloquy, and
that I do not dread to meet with unmerited reproach. And certain I am,
whensoever I shall be convinced the good of my country requires my reputation to be put in risk, regard for my own fame will not come in competition with an object of so much magnitude. . . To say more would be
indiscreet. . . You will perceive, my dear Sir, . . that my inclinations
will dispose and decide me to remain as I am, unless a clear and insur-
mountable conviction should be impressed on my mind, that some very
disagreeable consequences must, in all human probability, result from
the indulgence of my wishes."

SAME, TO COLONEL HAMILTON, *Oct.* 3d, 1788. — "In acknowledging the
receipt of your candid and kind letter by the last post, little more is
incumbent upon me than to thank you sincerely for the frankness with
which you communicated your sentiments, and to assure you that the
same manly tone of intercourse will always be more than barely welcome :
indeed, it will be highly acceptable to me. I am particularly glad in the
present instance, that you have dealt thus freely and like a friend.* . .
Situated as I am, I could hardly bring the question into the slightest
discussion, or ask an opinion even in the most confidential manner, without betraying, in my judgment, some impropriety of conduct. . . Now,
if I am not grossly deceived in myself, I should unfeignedly rejoice in
case the Electors, by giving their votes in favor of some other person,
would save me from the dreadful dilemma of being forced to accept or
refuse.

" If that may not be, . . I am truly solicitous to obtain all the
previous information, which the circumstances will afford, and to deter-
mine (when the determination can with propriety be no longer postponed)
according to the principles of right reason and the dictates of a clear
conscience, without too great a reference to the unforeseen consequences
which may affect my person or reputation. Until that period, I may
fairly hold myself open to conviction ; though I allow your sentiments to
have weight in them, and I shall not pass by your arguments without
giving them as dispassionate a consideration as I can possibly bestow. . .

" You will, I am well assured, believe the assertion, though I have little
expectation it would gain credit from those who are less acquainted with
me, that, if I should receive the appointment, and if I should be prevailed
upon to accept it, the acceptance would be attended with more diffidence and reluctance than I ever experienced before in my life. . .

* Referring to the reply of Colonel Hamilton to remarks in General Washington's
preceding letter of *Aug.* 28th, p. 77. The following is an abstract of that reply : — "I
should be deeply pained, my dear Sir, if your scruples in regard to a cert in station
should be matured into a resolution to decline it. . . It cannot be considered as a compliment, to say that on your acceptance of the office of President, the success of the new
Government in its commencement may materially depend. Your agency and influence
will be not less important in preserving it from future attacks of its enemies, than they
have been in recommending it in the first instance to the adoption of the people. . . In
a matter so essential to the well-being of society, as the prosperity of a newly institu'ed
Government, a citizen of so much consequence as yourself to its success. has no option
but to lend his services if called for. . . Your signature to the proposed System pledges
your judgment for its being such an one as you think the whole was worthy of the public
approbation. If it should miscarry (as men commonly decide from success or the want
of it), the blame will in all probability be laid upon the System itself.   .   .
"I will only add, that in my estimate of the matter, that [your] aid is indispensable.
. . I flatter myself the frankness with which I have delivered myself will not be dis-
pleasing to you. It has been prompted by motives which you would not disapprove."

" But why these anticipations? If the friends to the Constitution conceive that my administering it will be the means of its acceleration and strength, is it improbable that the adversaries of it may not ent rtain the same ideas, and of course make it an object of opposition? That many of this description will become Electors, I can have no doubt, any more than that their opposition will extend to any character, who, from whatever cause, would be likely to thwart their measures. It might be impolitic in them to make this declaration previous to the election ; but I shall be out in my conjectures if they do not act conformably thereto, and, if the seeming moderation, by which they appear to be actuated at present, is either more or less than a finesse to lull and deceive. Their plan of operations is systematized, and a regular intercourse, I have much reason to believe, between the leaders of it in the several States, is formed to render it more effectual." *

GENERAL WASHINGTON, to GENERAL LINCOLN, Oct. 26th, 1788. — "As the period is now rapidly approaching, which must decide the fate of the new Constitution, . . it is not wonderful that we should all feel an unusual degree of anxiety on the occasion. I must acknowledge my fears have been greatly alarmed, but still I am not without hopes. From the good beginning that has been made in Pennsylvania, a State from which much was to be feared, I cannot help anticipating well of the others. That is to say, I flatter myself a majority of them will appoint federal members to the several branches of the new Government. . . There will, however, be no reason for the advocates of the Constitution to relax in their exertions; for, if they should be lulled into security, appointments of anti-federal men may probably take place, and the consequences, which you so justly dread, be realized. . . Perhaps as much opposition. or, in other words, as great an effort for early amendments, is to be apprehended from this State as from any but New York. . . . .

" I would willingly pass over in silence that part of your letter in which you mention the persons who are candidates for the two first offices in the Executive, if I did not fear the omission might seem to betray a want of confidence. Motives of delicacy have prevented me hitherto from conversing or writing on the subject. whenever I could avoid it with decency. . . I must reserve to myself the right of making up my final decision at the last moment, when it can be brought into one view, and when the expediency or inexpediency of a refusal can be more judiciously determined than at present. . . . . . If, after all, I should conceive myself in a manner constrained to accept, I call Heaven to witness, that this very act would be the greatest sacrifice of my personal feelings and wishes, that ever I have been called upon to make. It would be to forego repose and domestic enjoyment, for trouble, perhaps for public obloquy ; for I should consider myself as entering upon an unexplored field, enveloped on every side with clouds and darkness." †

* To this letter, also, Colonel Hamilton replied. The following extract from his reply indicates no change in his sentiments respecting the main point of the discussion: — "I feel a conviction that you will finally see your acceptance to be indispensable. It is no compliment to say, that no other man can sufficiently unite the public opinion, or can give the requisite weight to the office in the commencement of the Government. These considerations appear to me of themselves decisive. I am not sure that your refusal would not throw everything into confusion. I am sure it would have the worst effect imaginable. Indeed, as I hinted in a former letter, I think circumstances leave no option."

† From General Lincoln's letter. — "The information which your Excellency has received respecting the machinations of the anti-federal characters, appears, from what circulates in this part of the country, but too well founded. I have no doubt but every exertion will be made to introduce into the new Government, in the first instance, characters unfriendly to those parts of it, which, in my opinion, are its brightest ornaments and its most precious jewels. To this they will be induced . . first, with a view totally to change the nature of the Government immediately. But, should they fail of that, they will then have it in their power to introduce into all the important offices in Government, men of their own sentiments ; so that in a short time, by their influence, they may bring about that change, which cannot at first or in any other way be effected by them. . . There never was an instance, when it could have been more necessary to call into exercise the wisdom, the prudence, and the patriotism, of the United States,

GENERAL WASHINGTON, to WILLIAM GORDON, in England, *Dec. 23d*, 1788.— — " The prospect, that a good General Government will, in all human probability, be soon established in America, affords me more substantial satisfaction than I have ever before derived from any political event ; because there is a rational ground for believing, that not only the happiness of my own countrymen, but that of mankind in general, will be promoted by it."

SAME, to the MARQUIS DE LAFAYETTE, *Jan. 29th,* 1789. — " The last letter, which I had the pleasure of writing to you, was forwarded by Mr. GOUVERNEUR MORRIS.* Since his departure from America, . . the minds of men have not been in a stagnant state ; but patriotism, instead of faction, has generally agitated them. . . The choice of Senators, Representatives, and Electors, which, excepting that of the last description, took place at different times in the different States, has afforded abundant topics for domestic news since the beginning of Autumn. . As I imagine you see most of the several particulars detailed in the American Gazettes, I will content myself with only saying, that the elections have been hitherto vastly more favorable than we could have expected ; that federal sentiments seem to be growing with uncommon rapidity, and that this increasing unanimity is not less indicative of the good disposition than of the good sense of the Americans. Did it not savor so much of partiality for my countrymen, I might add, that I cannot help flattering myself, that the new Congress, on account of the self-created respectability and various talents of its members, will not be inferior to any Assembly in the world. From these, and some other circumstances, I really entertain greater hopes that America will not finally disappoint the expectations of her friends, than I have at almost any former period.

than it will be in the important transactions of appointing the Executive and Legislative branches of the new Government. For the first impression made therein will probably give a tone to all future measures.

" We are happy here in finding it to be the unanimous voice of this rising Empire, that your Excellency, who has so just a claim to the merit of its establishment, should now take it under your protection. The share you hold in the affections of the people, and the unlimited confidence they place in your integrity and judgment, give you an elevated stand among them, which no other man can or probably ever will command. These things must insure to you all which a susceptible mind can wish, — a power of promoting in the highest degree the happiness of a virtuous and enlightened country.

" But will not these very important considerations alarm those anti-federal characters before mentioned ? . . .We must expect, and we should be guarded in every point to prevent, the influence of the intrigues and combinations of those, who wish to see every thing again afloat. They will endeavor, as one of the most probable means by which they may effect their purpose, to prevent your acceptance of the Presidency, your election they cannot hinder.

" I have, my dear General, thus freely written from the fullest conviction of duty, and in perfect confidence in your Excellency. I feel myself exceedingly interested to see such a Government, as we want and need, established without loss of time, . . I hope yet to live and enjoy the blessings of it. . . I wish to see a Government in existence, and properly administered, that I may not suffer the sad mortification, which would take place, if, after all the toils, dangers, and sufferings of a long and distressing war, prosecuted for the purpose of warding off an impending blow, and of establishing our country in those rights to which it was justly entitled, the people should, from any conduct of theirs, lose those blessings, to secure which, was the sole end of the important struggle."

* It is doubtless recollected that Mr. Morris was one of the most active and influential members of the Convention. In the prosecution of business engagements with Robert Morris he embarked on board a vessel for France, *Dec.* 18th, 1788, and was absent from the United States ten years. In a letter to him, *Nov.* 23th, prior to his departure for France, General Washington wrote, in reference to one previously received from Mr. Morris, — " As to what you hint respecting myself, towards the close of your letter, I have really but little leisure or inclination to enter on the discussion of a subject so unpleasant to me."

Mr. Morris rejoined, — " On the subject which has closed both your letter and mine, I feel too much not to say something. I have ever thought and said, that you *must* be President. No other man can fill that office. No other man can draw forth the abilities of our country into the various departments of civil life. You alone can awe the insolence of opposing factions, and the greater insolence of assuming adherents. . . You will become the father of more than three millions of children; and while *your* bosom glows with parental tenderness, in *theirs*, or at least a majority of them, you will excite the duteous sentiments of filial affection. . . I form my conclusions from those talents and virtues, which the world *believes*, and your friends *know* you possess," — *Philadelphia, Dec. 6th.*

Still, however, in such a fickle state of existence I would not be too sanguine. . . lest some unforeseen mischance or perverseness should occasion the greater mortification, by blasting the enjoyment in the very bud.

"I can say little or nothing new, in consequence of the repetition of your opinion, on the expediency there will be for my accepting the office to which you refer. Your sentiments, indeed, coincide much more nearly with those of my other friends than with my own feelings.* . . Should circumstances render it, in a manner, inevitably necessary, . be assured, my dear Sir, I shall assume the task with the most unfeigned reluctance, and with a real diffidence, for which I shall probably receive no credit from the world. If I know my own heart, nothing short of a conviction of duty will induce me again to take an active part in public affairs ; and in that case, if I can form a plan for my own conduct, my endeavors shall be unremittingly exerted, even at the hazard of former fame or present popularity, to extricate my country from the embarrassments in which it is entangled ; . . and to establish a general system of policy, which, if pursued, will ensure permanent felicity to the Commonwealth. I think I see a path as clear and as direct as a ray of light, which leads to the attainment of that object. Nothing but harmony, honesty, industry, and frugality, are necessary to make us a great and happy people. Happily, the present posture of affairs, and the prevailing disposition of my countrymen, promise to co-operate in establishing those four great and essential pillars of public felicity.

"While you are quarrelling among yourselves in Europe ; while one king is running mad, and others acting as if they were already so, by cutting the throats of the subjects of their neighbors ; I think you need not doubt, my dear Marquis, that we shall continue in tranquillity here, and that population will be progressive, so long as there shall continue to be so many easy means for obtaining a subsistence, and so ample a field for the exertion of talents and industry."

To Count de Rochambeau, he wrote, on the same day,—"We are on the point of seeing the completion of the new Government, which, by giving motives to labor, and security to property, cannot fail to augment, beyond all former example, the capital stock, that is to say, the aggregate amount of property in the country. I speak with the more confidence, because so many of the elections of Senators and Representatives to Congress are already made, that there is the best reason to believe the wisdom, the patriotism, and the virtue, of America will be conspicuously concentred in that body."

As would seem, no intelligent reader of the last preceding thirteen pages, could fail to believe that the emphatic expressions of increased hope and confidence in the last three extracts, were prompted by the apparent success of the earnest and indefatigable endeavors of the wisest patriots to secure a fair trial of the Constitution, in the same form and condition in which it was sent to Congress by the Convention.

* All public men, who enjoyed opportunities for sufficiently extended observation and experience, appear to have coincided in the opinion, that as an object of political necessity, General Washington *must* be the first President. Dr. Franklin, the most eminent among them, in a letter, *June 8th,* 1788, wrote,—"General Washington is the man that all our eyes are fixed on for President, and what little influence I may have is devoted to him."

Governor Johnson, of Maryland, wrote, *Oct. 10th,*—"We cannot, Sir, do without you; and I and thousands more can explain to anybody but yourself why we cannot do without you."

In consequence of the omission in the appropriate place, page 78, where Colonel Lee's name occurs, it seems due to truth to mention that he did not belong to the class of Lees referred to, page 72; but was distinguished for his efficient services as a cavalry officer during the Revolutionary war, and was a steadfast friend of the Constitution and of the policy of Washington.—Editor.

COMMENCEMENT OF THE NEW GOVERNMENT.

The commencement of a new Government, instituted BY AND FOR AN INTELLIGENT, A FREE, AND PROSPECTIVELY A GREAT AND HAPPY PEOPLE, was an event of such magnitude, and so obviously of immeasurable, — of absolutely vital interest and consequence to the whole and every part of the Nation, that some important facts, viewed in their connection with it, afford another illustration of the degenerate and relaxed state to which, as has been repeatedly shown, public sentiment had at that period been reduced. Concerning those facts, an opinion may be derived from the following description in the language of the late CHIEF JUSTICE MARSHALL: — *

"The impotence of the late Government [the Confederation], added to the dilatoriness inseparable from its perplexed mode of proceeding on the public business, and to its continued session, had produced among the members of Congress such an habitual disregard of punctuality in their attendance on that body, that, although the new Government was to commence its operations on the *4th* of *March*, 1789, a House of Representatives was not formed until the first, nor a Senate until the sixth, day of April.

"The ceremonies of inauguration having been adjusted by Congress, the President attended in the Senate-chamber on the 30th of April, in order to take, in the presence of both Houses, the oath prescribed by the Constitution.

"Having taken it in the view of an immense concourse of people, he delivered the address."

Whether or not the favorable results anticipated by GENERAL WASHINGTON, and by a majority of his countrymen, were realized from the operations of the new Government under his administration, may be inferred from the following extracts : —

In a letter to GOUVERNEUR MORRIS, *Oct.* 13*th*, 1789, PRESIDENT WASHINGTON wrote : —" That the *national* Government is organized, and, as far as my information goes, to the satisfaction of all parties ; that opposition is either no more, or hides its head ; that it is hoped and expected it will take strong root, and that the non-acceding States [North Carolina and Rhode Island] will very soon become members of the Union."

In MR. MORRIS's Reply, dated PARIS, *Jan.* 24*th*, 1790, he wrote : — " It gave me very sincere pleasure to learn from *you* the good tidings, which you communicated respecting our new form of Government. . . I have from time to time received very great pleasure, at the development of its

---

* Marshall's Washington, in two volumes, vol. 2, pp. 138, 146.

As nearly all the extracts from letters of Washington, have been taken from his Writings in twelve volumes, edited by the late Dr. Sparks, their several places are indicated by their dates.
Likewise those, from Mr. Jefferson's letters in his Works in four volumes, are indicated in the same manner.

principles by the Legislature, which in my opinion does them the greatest
honor. They have far, very far, outgone my expectations, and even come
up, not only to my hopes, but to my very wishes. . . I hope in God,
my dear Sir, that you will long continue to preside, and that not only
you, but all who succeed you, may be assisted by counsellors as able and
honest, as those who now fill the different seats in Congress. The prospect
of public felicity, which must be the result, fills my bosom with delight.
O my country, how happy! didst thou but know thy blessedness."

PRESIDENT WASHINGTON, TO MRS. CATHARINE MACAULAY GRAHAM, *Jan. 9th*,
1790. — "If, after all my humble but faithful endeavors to advance the
felicity of my country and mankind, I may indulge a hope, that my
labors have not been altogether without success, it will be the only real
compensation I can receive in the closing scenes of life.

"On the actual situation of this country under its new Government, I
will make a few remarks. That the Government, though not actually
perfect, is one of the best in the world, I have little doubt. . . . It
was indeed next to a miracle, that there should have been so much unanimity in points of so great importance among such a number of citizens,
so widely scattered, and so different in their habits in many respects, as
the Americans were. Nor are the growing unanimity and increasing good
will of the citizens to the Government less remarkable, than [those]
favorable circumstances.

"So far as we have gone with the new Government (and it is completely
organized and in operation), we have had greater reason than the most
sanguine could expect, to be satisfied with its success. The increase of
commerce is visible in every port, and the number of new manufactures
introduced in one year is astonishing. I have lately made a tour through
the Eastern States. I found the country in a great degree recovered from
the ravages of the war ; the towns flourishing, and the people delighted
with a Government instituted by themselves, and for their own good. The
same facts, I have also reason to believe from good authority, exist in the
Southern States.

"By what I have just observed, I think you will be persuaded that the
ill-boding politicians, who prognosticated that America never would enjoy
any fruits from her Independence, and that she would be obliged to
have recourse to foreign power for protection, have at least been mistaken.
I shall sincerely rejoice to see, that the American Revolution has been
productive of happy consequences on both sides of the Atlantic."

SAME, to CHARLES PINCKNEY, of S.C., *Jan. 11th*, 1790. — "My late tour
through the Eastern States has been of salutary consequence in confirming
my health. I have likewise had an opportunity of seeing how far the
country has recovered from the ravages of the war, and how well the
inhabitants are disposed to support the General Government."

SAME, to the MARQUIS DE LA LUZERNE, *April 29th*, 1790. — "I am much
pleased with the interest you take in our *national* reputation ; and the
information you give, that our credit is becoming respectable in Europe,
under the influence of our new Government."

SAME, to the MARQUIS DE LAFAYETTE, *June 3d*, 1790. — "You have
doubtless been informed, from time to time, of the happy progress of our
affairs. The principal difficulties which oppose themselves in any shape
to the prosperous execution of our Government, seem in a great measure to
have been surmounted. A good temper prevails among our citizens. . .
"Our Government is now happily carried into operation. Although some
thorny questions still remain, it is to be hoped that the wisdom of those
concerned in the *national* Legislature will dispose of them prudently. A
funding system is one of the subjects which occasions most anxiety and
perplexity. Yet our revenues have been considerably more productive
than it was imagined they would be . . Our trade to the East India
flourishes. The profits to individuals are so considerable as to induce more
persons to engage in it continually."

SAME, to DAVID STEWART, *June 15th*, 1790.—" Our reputation has risen in every part of the globe ; and our credit, especially in Holland, where our funds are above par. has got higher than that of any nation in Europe, as appears by official advices just received." *

SAME, to THOMAS MARSHALL [of Kentucky], *Feb. 6th*, 1791. — " I never doubted. that the operations of this Government, if not perverted by prejudice or evil designs, would inspire the citizens of America with such confidence in it, as effectually to do away those apprehensions, which, under the former, our best men entertained of divisions among ourselves, or allurements from other nations. I am therefore happy to find that such a disposition prevails in your part of the country, as to remove any idea of that evil, which a few years ago you so much dreaded."

SAME, to the MARQUIS DE LAFAYETTE, *March 19th*, 1791. — " Our country, my dear Sir (and it is truly *yours*), is fast advancing in its political importance and social happiness. . . The laws of the United States, adapted to the public exigencies, are framed with wisdom, and acquiesced in with cheerfulness. The administration of them, aided by the affectionate partiality of my countrymen, is attended with no unnecessary inconvenience, and every circumstance is auspicious to your fellow-citizens in this section of the globe."

SAME, to MRS. CATHARINE MACAULAY GRAHAM,† *July 19th*, 1791.—" I shall only further add, what I know will give you pleasure, that the United States enjoy a scene of prosperity and tranquillity under the new Government, that could hardly have been hoped for under the old ; and that, while you, in Europe, are troubled.with war and rumors of war, every one here may sit under his own vine, and none to molest or make him afraid."

SAME, to DAVID HUMPHREYS, *July 20th*, 1791. — " Each day's experience of the Government of the United States seems to confirm its establishment, and to render it more popular. A ready acquiescence in the laws made under it, shows in a strong light the confidence which the people have in their Representatives, and in the upright views of those who administer the Government. . . Our public credit stands on that ground, which three years ago it would have been a species of madness to have foretold. The astonishing rapidity with which the newly instituted bank was filled, gives an unexampled proof of the resources of our countrymen, and their confidence in public measures. On the first day of opening the subscription, the whole number of shares (twenty thousand) were taken up in one hour, and application made for upwards of four thousand more than were granted by the institution, besides many others that were coming in from different quarters." ‡

SAME, to the MARQUIS DE LAFAYETTE, *July 28th*, 1791. — " On the sixth of this month I returned from a tour through the Southern States. . . In the course of this journey, I have been highly gratified in observing the flourishing state of the country, and the good dispositions of the people. Industry and economy have become very fashionable in those parts, which were formerly noted for the opposite qualities. The attachment of all classes of citizens to the General Government seems to be a pleasing presage of their future happiness and respectability.

" The complete establishment of our public credit is a strong mark of the confidence of the people, in the virtue of their Representatives, and the

---

* Previous to the new Government, claims against the United States had depreciated to one eighth of their nominal value.

† This letter was not received by Mrs. Graham. She died, *June 22nd*, 1791.

‡ He wrote to Count de Moustier, *Sept. 5th*. — " The favorable sentiments which you express of our country and its councils are very agreeable to me.
" You will learn with pleasure, that events have realized the most sanguine hopes of national prosperity. The influence of the General Government has extended to every relation of political improvement, and to the promotion of our social happiness."

wisdom of their measures. . . This contrast between the situation of the people of the United States and those of Europe, is too striking to be passed over, even by the most superficial observer. . . But we do not wish to be the only people, who may taste the sweets of an equal and good Government. We look with an anxious eye to the time when happiness and tranquillity shall prevail in your country, and when all Europe shall be freed from commotions, tumults and alarms.''

SAME, to GOUVERNEUR MORRIS, *July 28th*, 1791. — '' Dear Sir, — The communications in your several letters, relative to the state of affairs in Europe, are very gratefully received. . .

'' The change of systems, which have so long prevailed in Europe, will undoubtedly affect us in a degree proportioned to our political or commercial connections with the several nations of it. . . The present moment seems pregnant with great events. . . That a change there will be favorable to this country, I have no doubt. For under the former system we were seen either in the distresses of war, or viewed after the peace in a most unfavorable light through the medium of our distracted state. In neither point could we appear of much consequence among nations. . . A change of system will open a new view of things, and we shall then burst upon them, as it were, with redoubled advantages. . .

'' In my late tour through the Southern States, I experienced great satisfaction in seeing the good effects of the General Government in that part of the Union. The people at large have felt the security which it gives, and the equal justice which it administers to them. The farmer, the merchant, and the mechanic, have seen their several interests attended to, and thence they unite in placing a confidence in their Representatives, as well as in those in whose hands the execution of the laws is placed. Industry has there taken place of idleness, and economy, of dissipation. . . The establishment of public credit is an immense point gained in our *national* concerns. This, I believe, exceeds the expectation of the most sanguine among us.''

SAME, to the MARQUIS DE LAFAYETTE, *June 10th*, 1792. — '' The affairs of the United States still go on in a prosperous train. We increase daily in numbers and riches, and the people are blessed with the enjoyment of those rights, which alone can give security and happiness to a Nation.''

After seeing how essential interests are affected by the nature of a Government resting on the BALLOT, who can doubt the need of regarding the distinctive nature of that system of Government called the Confederation, whose results are shown in pp. 11–14, and often declared in the Convention, and of then noticing the perfect contrast between those results and the true developments from the unperverted operations of the new System called the Constitution, as these developments are seen through the extracts in pp. 83–86 ?

If any one, who has learned these opposite lessons from the Fathers, will add the teachings derivable from his past and present observations of public affairs, and from the contents of the pages in this Work complete, he may be able to judge with much confidence, whether there is now, or ever has been since the beginning of the Union, as strong a tendency to a possibly dangerous consolidation, as to a probably entire and final destruction of all the great interests, and consequently of the long-cherished hopes and expectations, of United America. In this connection is suggested the Inquiry, — By whose agencies and influences was National Liberty gained, and, afterward, so far regulated and secured as to have been defended and preserved to the present time ?